From Darkness to Light

Divine Love and the Transmutation of Evil

RON MACFARLANE

Copyright © 2016 Ron MacFarlane

All rights reserved.

Published 2016 by
Greater Mysteries Publications
Mission, BC, Canada

Cover Design: Ron MacFarlane

Printed in the United States of America

ISBN:
ISBN-13: 978-0994007759
ISBN-10: 0994007752

DEDICATION

This work is reverently dedicated to St. Michael the Archai, who has faithfully served the God of Love throughout the long planetary ages; and who has unwaveringly opposed the cosmic dragon of evil in order to protect nascent humanity from descending into the infernal abyss of
spiritual darkness.

CONTENTS

Introduction i

Chapter 1 A Brief Background to Understanding Evil
1.1 The Decline of the Word "Evil" in Modern Society 1
1.2 The Ancient Recognition of Evil 3
1.3 What Evil Originally Meant in Ancient Times 5
1.4 Evil as Understood by Ancient Judaism 6
1.5 Evil as Understood by Early Christianity 8
1.6 Evil Does Not Exist Without God 9

Chapter 2 The Nature, Genesis and Consequences of Evil
2.1 Evil Can Only Occur Within the Created Universe 11
2.2 Evil Can Only Occur with Sentient-Beings Who Possess Free-Will 12
2.3 Evil, as "Ungodly Will-Power," Originates in the Soul 13
2.4 Minerals, Plants and Animals are Incapable of Evil 13
2.5 Manifestations and Consequences of Evil, Particularly Sin 14
2.6 The Many Unfortunate Consequences of Sin, Including Hell 15

Chapter 3 Fallacious Conceptions and the Purpose of Evil
3.1 Matter Itself is Not Intrinsically Evil 17
3.2 Correcting the Faulty Logic Which Concludes That Evil Does Not Exist 18
3.3 Refuting the Misconception that "Good Does Not Exist Without Evil" 20
3.4 The Faulty Concept: "Good Can Come From Evil" 20
3.5 Are Disasters Such as Tornadoes, Hurricanes, Earthquakes and Floods "Natural Evils"? 21
3.6 The Erroneous Conception that "Free-Will Cannot Exist Without Evil" 22
3.7 The Faulty Concept: "Without Evil There is No Freedom" 24

Chapter 4	**Supernatural Perpetrators of Evil: Lucifer**	
4.1	Know Your Enemy	27
4.2	Lucifer: Mankind's Initial Encounter with Evil	29
4.3	Lucifer's Mistaken Understanding of Freedom	32
4.4	Recognizing Lucifer's Evil Agenda for the Future	34
4.5	Lemurian Humanity's Fall from Paradise	35
4.6	Lucifer's Love of Self and Overwhelming Pride	36
4.7	Lucifer's Lemurian Assault on Sensory Perception and Standing Upright	37
4.8	Lucifer's Atlantean Assault on the Vital Organs and Speech	39
4.9	The Physical Incarnation of Lucifer in Ancient China	42
4.10	Lucifer's Attack on Human Thinking During the Graeco-Roman Cultural Era	43
4.11	Assessing Lucifer's Legacy of Evil Interference	44
Chapter 5	**Supernatural Perpetrators of Evil: Ahriman**	
5.1	Ahriman: Mankind's Second Encounter with Evil	47
5.2	Understanding Ahriman, the "Unlawful Prince of this World"	48
5.3	Ahriman's Early Evil Interferences	51
5.4	Ahriman's Increasing Evil Influence in the Modern Era	53
5.5	The Destined Physical Incarnation of Ahriman	56
5.6	Ahriman Appearing as the Jewish Messiah and the Christian Parousia	59
5.7	Has Ahriman's Premature Incarnation in 1998 Been Successfully Averted?	61
Chapter 6	**Supernatural Perpetrators of Evil: Sorath**	
6.1	Sorath: Mankind's Third Encounter with Evil	63
6.2	Delving into the Evil Nature of the Sun-Demon	65
6.3	Sorath: The Two-Horned Beast of Atlantean Black-Magic	67
6.4	Sorathic Black-Magic in the Post-Atlantean Age	70
6.5	Sorath and the Infernal Circle of Twelve	75
6.6	Sorath and the Sub-Surface Etheric Realm of Agharti	78

Chapter 7		The Inverse Triad of Evil: Lucifer, Ahriman and Sorath	
	7.1	The Great Universal Law of Triplicity	79
	7.2	The Universal Principle of Rhythm: The Forces of Expansion, Contraction and Equilibrium	80
	7.3	The Universal Principle of Vibration	82
	7.4	The Cosmic Manifestation of Universal Mind	83
	7.5	Universal Mind as a Lower Vibration of Universal Being	87
	7.6	Universal Being as a Lower Vibration of Spirit	88
	7.7	The One God as a Unified Trinity of Divine Persons	90
	7.8	The Inverse Triad of Evil	93
Chapter 8		Celestial Benefactors of Mankind: The Solar-Christos	
	8.1	The Foremost Benefactor of Mankind: The Solar-Christos	95
	8.2	The Solar-Christos and Lucifer are *Not* Celestial Brothers	98
	8.3	The Solar-Christos is Already Victorious Over the Evil Triad of Lucifer, Ahriman and Sorath.	101
	8.4	The Solar-Christos as the Harmonizing Protection from the Extremes of Evil	104
	8.5	Mankind Does Not Need Lucifer, Ahriman or Sorath in Order to Exist in the World	106
	8.6	An Alternative to the "Polar-Opposite Method" of Counterbalancing Lucifer and Ahriman	107
	8.7	Avoiding the Evil Excesses in Life by Focusing on the Divine Trinity	109
	8.8	Achieving Spiritual Balance and Equipoise by Centering on Christ-Jesus	110
	8.9	The Harmonizing Radiance of Christ-Jesus From the Sacred Cube of the Heart	111

Chapter 9 Celestial Benefactors of Mankind: Yahweh-Elohim

9.1 Yahweh-Elohim: The Advanced Leader of the Angelic Kingdom ... 115
9.2 Yahweh-Elohim and the Formation of the Moon ... 116
9.3 Yahweh-Elohim and the Anti-Luciferic Functions of Heredity and Tribal Love ... 117
9.4 Under the Direction of Christ-Jesus, Yahweh-Elohim Now Promotes True, Personal Freedom ... 118
9.5 Yahweh-Elohim's Mission to Prepare the Ancient Hebrews for the Birth of the Messiah ... 121
9.6 Yahweh-Elohim as the Principal Embodiment of the Holy Mother-Spirit for the Third Hierarchy ... 123

Chapter 10 Celestial Benefactors of Mankind: Michael the Archai

10.1 St. Michael: The Great Opponent of the Dragon of Evil ... 125
10.2 Michael as Mankind's Guardian of Spiritual Truth ... 126
10.3 Spiritual Science as a Modern-Day Initiative of Michael ... 127
10.4 Michael as the New Herald and Guardian of the Etheric Christ-Jesus ... 129
10.5 The Power of Michael Casts Out Ahrimanic Fear, Hatred and Anxiety from Within the Human Body ... 131
10.6 Michael: Guardian Knight of the Universal Woman ... 132

Conclusion Moving Positively Into the Future

C.1 Salvation From Supernatural Evil is a Free-Will Choice ... 135
C.2 The Tragic Irony of Evil: Opposing God is Opposing One's Own True Self ... 136
C.3 Divine Love is the Best Way of Dealing with Evil ... 136

Notes ... 141

Select Bibliography ... 159

FROM DARKNESS
TO LIGHT

INTRODUCTION

IN THE LIGHT of spiritual science, never before in the history of the world has there been such an assailment of supernatural evil upon humanity as extensive and intense as there exists at the present time. Subconsciously pouring into the human soul are the seductive whisperings of Luciferic beings and fallen angels; the perceptual distortions of Ahrimanic (Satanic) beings; the lurid, egocentric promptings of corrupt spirits of personality (asuras); and the violent inducements of blood-lust rising up from the subterranean "beast of Revelation" (Sorath the sun-demon).

The tragic and bitter irony of all this, however, is that because of today's pervasive, atheistic and secular culture and the materialistic worldview of natural science, individual human beings are correspondingly the most oblivious to supernatural evil than they have ever been at any other time in world history.

To be sure, people today are certainly aware of the *effects* of supernatural evil—extensive and increased natural disasters; horrific instances of mass genocide; the prolific use of torture and brutality by government agencies; individual acts of sudden cruelty and murder; pathological selfishness throughout the world's business and financial markets;

strange, globally-infectious viral contagions; the devaluation of human life through abortion and euthanasia; and a worldwide pandemic of dehumanizing drug addiction. What most people today fail to realize is that the invisible fomenting agents—the *causes*—of all these life-threatening, destructive physical events and pathologies are ultimately rooted in the impulses of supernatural evil.

To be sure, mankind would have completely and totally succumbed to this tsunami of supernatural evil if it weren't for the protective and opposing intervention of powerful, benevolent celestial beings, such as St. Michael the Archai, Yahweh-Elohim (the spirit of the moon), and the Solar-Christos (aka: "Christ"—the regent of the sun).

More than ever, it is crucially important in today's world to understand the nature of evil, and to become more aware and cognizant of the various perpetrators of supernatural evil. Thereby, conscious cooperation with the compassionate protectors and guardians of mankind can be increased and strengthened, so that supernatural evil is better resisted and eventually overcome.

To this end, *From Darkness to Light: Divine Love and the Transmutation of Evil* delves deeply into the thorny questions of "What exactly is evil?", together with "How and when did evil begin?", as well as "Why does God allow evil to exist?" Once the nature, genesis and purpose of evil is better understood, then various influential superphysical perpetrators of supernatural evil will be examined in closer detail. Correspondingly, the superphysical proponents of cosmic holiness will be identified and better understood as well.

Wherever possible, the spiritual-scientific research of anthroposophy—an independent offshoot of the Rosicrucian Fraternity, and the modern-day expression of esoteric Christianity that was established by Rudolf Steiner (1861–1925)—will be included and referenced. Following this profoundly-esoteric background, the destined human struggle with continuing and obdurate evil—far into the future development of the earth—will also be mentally envisioned and supersensibly examined.

It is sincerely intended that upon completion of the entire written discourse, concerned individuals will be better armed and shielded in order to become actively engaged on the side of holiness and spiritual light in the prolonged cosmic battle against evil and material darkness.

CHAPTER 1

A BRIEF BACKGROUND TO UNDERSTANDING EVIL

1.1 The Decline of the Word "Evil" in Modern Society

IN A CURIOUSLY-GRADUAL and subtly-unnoticed way, the word "evil" has almost disappeared from common, everyday use in today's conversation and communication (at least in Western society). Someone like Adolf Hitler (1889–1945), for example, is now more likely to be described as a psychopath, a sociopath, a megalomaniac, a brutal dictator, an anti-Semitic demagogue, a fanatic or even a monster, rather than described as an "evil" personality.

Moreover, the most heinous crimes in today's world news are more likely to be described as atrocities, brutalities, radicalizations, genocides, barbarities, villainies, cruelties, savageries, terrorism or even insanities, rather than as "evil" events. Perhaps the most noticeable exception to this widespread word-avoidance in recent decades has been by US government officials. In 1983, for instance, then US President

A BRIEF BACKGROUND TO UNDERSTANDING EVIL

Ronald Reagan (1911-2004) famously described the former Soviet Union as an "evil empire"; and also referred to the nuclear arms race as a struggle between "good and evil." Later in 2001, US President George W. Bush (b.1946) described Islamic terrorists as "evil-doers"; and in 2002 he referred to Iran, Iraq and North Korea as the "Axis of Evil."

No doubt the primary reason that "evil" was still a part of the Reagan and Bush vocabularies was because both American presidents were fundamentalist-style Christians who tend to view and describe the entire world in polarized "black and white" terminology; such as "us and them," "right and wrong," "good and evil." In fact, one can readily generalize that the word "evil" is only used in today's world by those individuals who profess a religious belief in God. Atheistic-minded individuals are far less likely to view the world in terms of good and evil, and hence are far less inclined to use the word "evil" in describing persons and events. Since the atheistic, materialistic worldview of modern science has become so globally persuasive and pervasive, it is therefore not too surprising that the word "evil" is fast disappearing from the vocabulary of everyday conversation.

Equally curious, however, is the enormous worldwide popularity of movies, television shows, books and artwork that depict a cosmic battle between the forces of good and the forces of evil. The multi-billion dollar success of the December 2015 movie release of "Star Wars: The Force Awakens" is itself ample evidence of this popularity. So, how does one explain the current global tendency to increasingly disregard the real world in terms of good and evil, with the corresponding worldwide popularity of entertainment that portrays a cosmic battle of good versus evil?

No doubt, atheistic intellectuals could formulate some clever explanations for this apparent contradiction; but from a spiritual point of view, even though the atheistic worldview of materialistic science has stifled the conscious perception of a supernatural struggle between good and evil, subconsciously individuals today still instinctually sense that they are an integral part of an unseen spiritual conflict. As a result, this subconscious sensing rises up into everyday consciousness in the form of vivid dreams, pictorial images, dramatic stories, and artistic expressions.

1.2 The Ancient Recognition of Evil

In ancient times, no one doubted the existence of evil. Prior to modern times, there was no such thing as a secular, non-religious society—*all* were sacred societies that unquestioningly recognized the existence of a supernatural dimension wherein good battled against evil. This supernatural struggle was perceived to spill over into the natural world and into human affairs.

In ancient Persia, for example, the religion of Zoroaster (or Zarathustra) envisioned the entire cosmos that was created by the supreme being, Ahura Mazdao, as a battleground between two equally-powerful but opposing super-celestial spirits: Spenta Mainyu—the spirit of good who promoted "asha" (truth, order, justice and light), and Angra Mainyu—the spirit of evil who amplified "druj" (falsehood, disorder, injustice and darkness). Angra Mainyu was later personified as the devil-figure, Ahriman. In Zoroastrian tradition, mankind was expected to actively participate in the continuing conflict between good and evil, truth and falsehood.

In the Hindu religion of ancient India, even though an underlying cosmic polarity of good and evil was not necessarily envisioned, there was certainly a delineation of masculine and feminine divinities into two major categories: (1) "devas" or good gods, and (2) "asuras" or evil gods. Hindu epic poetry often described the famous battles that took place between the two sides; such as the defeat of the evil-asura Ravana, by the deva-hero Rama and his monkey-god assistant Hanuman. Ancient Hinduism also held that on occasion the gods would directly intervene in human affairs; such as the divine-avatar Krishna appearing to the human Arjuna in order to strengthen him in battle. It was further understood in Vedic literature that various devas and asuras manifested in the forces of nature and in human morality. The god Agni, for example, was seen as the spirit of fire, and the god Mitra was understood as the spirit of honesty and friendship.

As did ancient Hinduism, the religion of old Egypt envisioned a universe brimming with a pantheon of supernatural deities who personified important natural and human phenomena. The elongated body of the goddess Nut, for example, was regarded as the overarching sky who repeatedly swallowed up the setting sun-god Ra each evening, and who then gave birth to him anew each morning. Ma'at was the name of the supreme Egyptian goddess of truth and justice who embodied the essential harmony of the universe. Her supernatural power regulated the seasons and the movement of the stars. She was also the ultimate moral judge in the afterlife, where the heart of the newly-deceased was weighed against her feather of truth. A virtuous life gave levity to the heart, whereas wickedness weighed the heart down.

While most of the Egyptian gods and goddesses assisted Ma'at in maintaining the cosmic order, there were a few, particularly the god Seth, who were considered evil, and who were despised by the other deities. The evil Seth was the personification of darkness, chaos and confusion. Even though Horus, the deific personification of the sun-suffused atmosphere, was said to have defeated Seth, it was also understood that their battle was more of an eternal struggle between good and evil.

There were also a number of demon-beings associated with the Egyptian pantheon of deities. Even though these evil spirits were inferior to the gods and goddesses, they were still much more powerful than human beings, and who could therefore affect nature and humanity in a number of supernatural ways. One of the most prominent demons, Apep (or Apophis), continually opposed Ma'at (the cosmic order), and since he also fought against the light, he was given the title, "The Enemy of Ra." Being portrayed as a gigantic, subterranean serpent also gave Apep the title of "Evil Lizard."

Closer to the present day, the worldview of the classical Greeks was also populated with a myriad of supernatural beings, both good and evil. Numerous stygian deities, as well as semi-divine evil-spirits called "kakodaimons," inhabited the Grecian underworld; spirits such as Epiales, the underworld spirit of nightmares; Erebus, the primeval god of darkness; the Keres, horrible she-daimons who were responsible for violent death and disease; Tartarus, the primeval god of the infernal, subterranean pit below Hades; and Thanatus, the winged daimon of death.

Even though any number of ancient cultures can be similarly examined, it is clearly unnecessary to do so in order to accurately conclude that when evil was first formulated as a human concept and used as a spoken word (in whatever language), it was in connection with supernatural deities and spirit-beings. The question to pursue now is: "What is the connection between evil and the divine?"

1.3 What Evil Originally Meant in Ancient Times

According to the research of spiritual science, though our ancient ancestors lacked a well-defined sense of self and the ability to perform abstract intellection, they did possess an innate, dreamy clairvoyance that perceived the surrounding supernatural world in ephemeral picture images. Unfortunately, materialistic thinkers of today all too readily dismiss the mythologies and religious worldviews of the past as simply anthropomorphic imaginations that were primitive, superstitious attempts to explain the complex and frightening natural world. While supersensible research does recognize that a high degree of fanciful embellishment was certainly involved, the worldwide, cross-cultural accounts about supernatural beings and divinities in the past were not creative inventions; but were, in fact, the result of actual clairvoyant perception.

Nascent, undeveloped humanity actually beheld the beings and events of the supernatural world in an ethereal, dream-like way. The dimly-perceived spiritual beings who comforted and assisted struggling mankind also instilled order and balanced-harmony to the world; while the others who brought harm, injury and destruction to mankind were also perceived to be promoting disorder and chaos in the world. To our ancient ancestors, then, evil was not simply what brought harm, injury and destruction to human beings; but was also that which actively opposed the divinely-instilled order and harmony of the world. Moreover, evil spirits were also perceived to induce, instigate and instill evil activity in human beings as well as in the natural world.

When evil was first formulated and conceived by primeval mankind, then, it was in relation to a worldview that clairvoyantly perceived a natural world that was supernaturally suffused with divine beings and discarnate spirits. Simply stated, evil was understood as the shadow opposite of the good divinities; that is, as the willful actions of human and supernatural beings which brought injury and disorder to the divinely-formulated world.

1.4 Evil as Understood by Ancient Judaism

Ancient religions and mythologies were characteristically "polytheistic"; that is, they believed in multiple deities that were often organized into a pantheon of gods and goddesses. Ancient Judaism was of course a notable exception. Prior to the Old Testament patriarch Abraham (around 1813 BC), however, the ancestral Israelites were also recognized to be polytheists; or in the derogatory words of the Jewish *Hagadah*, they were "idol worshippers." Post-Abrahamic Judaism, however, was characteristically "monotheist"; that is, religious belief was restricted to only one God—a single divine being known as Yahweh.

Even though ancient Judaism acknowledged and worshipped only one God, it also continued to recognize a surrounding supernatural (or heavenly) realm that was inhabited by numerous superphysical beings. In this case, the heavenly-beings were not regarded as gods and goddesses; but rather as different kinds of angels who were also created by the one God.

Ancient Judaism did not perceive the world as an intrinsic, dualistic battleground between good and evil; but instead as the good creation of a good God. Nevertheless, so that created beings (humans and angels) learned to appreciate the gratuitous gift of world-existence, Yahweh-God encouraged freedom of choice; that is, the opportunity to choose between good and evil. "Choosing good" (or yetzer tov) was freely abiding by the will of God and obeying his commandments. "Choosing evil"—also known as an "evil inclination" (or yetzer ra)—was purposely defying the will of God and disobeying his commandments.

Though ancient Judaism did not acknowledge a class of "fallen" angels who were cast down to earth after losing a war in heaven (an angelic rebellion against God), there were familiar stories of angels, such as Azazel and Samhazai, who willingly descended to earth, and there became corrupted by sensual temptation. Moreover, "Ha-Satan" ('the Adversary') in Old Testament times was not regarded as the Devil, or an evil angel; but rather, as a specified angel instructed by Yahweh to tempt mankind to choose evil—to disregard the will of God and to disobey his commandments. As such, Ha-Satan was regarded as the personification of *the* evil inclination, and thereby also referred to as "Yetzer Harah." According to the *Torah* and *Midrashim*, the serpent in the Genesis garden of Eden was Ha-Satan.

1.5 Evil as Understood by Early Christianity

In early Christianity, evil became much more focused and personified in the figure of Satan—the Devil. Satan was understood to be a highly-advanced angel-being, originally named Lucifer (or "Light-Bearer"), who led a large-scale but unsuccessful rebellion of angels against God in heaven. As a result, Lucifer was stripped of his heavenly light and cast down with his companion "fallen" angels to the earth; thereby becoming Satan, the evil "god of this world" and the spirit of darkness, destruction and death.

Unlike ancient Judaism, Satan was not seen as an obedient angelic-agent of God; but instead as a powerful and widely-influential, superphysical opponent and enemy. Though Satan was perceived as good in the beginning, for some unknown reason he decided to choose evil—which was still understood by early Christianity to be the deliberate opposition to the will of God and the chosen disobedience of his commandments. By enduringly choosing evil, Satan became the superphysical embodiment of evil, and thereby the foremost supernatural source of evil for nascent and vulnerable mankind.

As the seductive, serpentine tempter in primeval paradise, Satan persuaded humanity's ancestral parents (Adam and

Eve) to disobey God's strict commandment not to partake of the fruit of knowledge from the tree of good and evil. This initial evil—which caused "original sin"—was perceived to have seriously and lastingly damaged humanity's pristine immortal nature; thereby resulting in an expulsion from paradise, and the beginning of pain, suffering, illness and death.

1.6 Evil Does Not Exist Without God

From what has been examined so far, it is readily apparent that mankind's perception and understanding of evil has remained remarkably consistent and unchanged throughout ancient time: evil was regarded as the deliberate defiance of the will of God (or gods), and the knowing rejection of his (or their) commandments. From this notion of evil, we can conclude that even though God can logically exist in his singular, infinite goodness without evil, it is obvious that evil cannot exist without God. If there were no God, then there could be no opposition to God, and therefore no evil.

From this we can better comprehend why the word "evil" is slowly disappearing from everyday use in today's increasingly secular and atheistic culture. If more and more people do not acknowledge a God of all-goodness, then they can't logically recognize evil as the defiance of God.

Without God-acknowledgement, any atheistic use of the word "evil" dilutes and alters the original meaning. For example, the word evil is often used nowadays to describe anything that is harmful or which causes injury to a person; such as the "evil of alcoholism," or the "social evil" of drug use, or the "natural evil" of tornadoes in America, or "That evil cat of mine scratched me again!" Moreover, government officials are also quick to use the word evil to describe foreign nations that are considered enemy states (as quoted earlier with US presidents Reagan and Bush). Over the years, unscrupulous governments have found that "demonizing" an enemy country or an enemy group (such as Islamic "terrorists") makes it much easier to declare war and then to "morally" engage in deadly military conflict with them.

Unfortunately, in the same way that denying the reality of God does not mean that he ceases to exist, denying the reality of evil also means that it does not cease to exist. Being blind to the causes and effects of evil in our world only strengthens its unseen, covert activity in our midst. In consequence, humanity unknowingly becomes easy prey to invisible agents of evil, instead of actively opposing and vanquishing them.

CHAPTER 2

THE NATURE, GENESIS AND
CONSEQUENCES OF EVIL

2.1 Evil Can Only Occur Within the Created Universe

UNDERSTANDING EVIL AS "the deliberate opposition to the will of God and the knowing disobedience to his commandments" may initially appear to be an oversimplistic explanation; when in fact it is necessary to delve very deeply into esoteric knowledge in order to understand what is meant by "God," the "will of God," "opposition," "deliberate," "knowing disobedience" and "his commandments."

God, as recognized in esoteric wisdom, is the one and only reality. This reality is all there is, complete in itself, infinite and eternal. Moreover, the one reality that is God possesses unlimited being, consciousness and life. "Good" is a term that describes the essential nature of God, which is divine love.

The universe is understood to be a temporal and finite creation of God, brought into existence by an exercise of his omnipotent will. The divine will, then, logically transcends the entire universe, and is the ultimate source of all power in creation.

Prior to creation, when God was content in himself, all was good; there was no evil. Since evil arises from opposing the divine will, and since God cannot logically oppose his own will, evil cannot and does not exist within the divine nature. It is only within the created universe that evil is possible. The penetrating question to answer now is: "How does evil arise within creation; that is, how is it possible to oppose the will of God in creation?"

2.2 Evil Can Only Occur with Sentient-Beings Who Possess Free-Will

"The deliberate opposition to the will of God" as a criterion of evil indicates that a conscious choice is involved; that is, in order to qualify as evil, there must be an intentional decision to oppose the will of God. Since the ability to freely and consciously choose one thing or another is only possessed by sentient-beings, evil could *not* occur within the created universe until sentient-beings with free-will came into existence.

This logical assertion has long been allegorically conveyed in the biblical book of Genesis where: "In the beginning God created the heavens and the earth ... And God saw everything that he had made, and behold, it was very good (Gen 1:1, 31). It was not until human beings came into existence, and then knowingly disobeyed the divine command to "not eat the fruit of the tree of knowledge of good and evil," that evil occurred.

Also noteworthy, according to the Genesis account, evil did not begin with human beings; but rather, it had already existed prior to "the disobedience of Adam and Eve." By persuading our naïve and gullible human ancestors to disobey God's commandment, the serpent (that is, Lucifer/Satan) was already engaging in evil activity. Even from this brief biblical incident, it can be reasonably surmised that created angel-beings also possessed the capacity of free-will, and that some had already chosen to engage in evil prior to the emergence of human beings.

2.3 Evil, as "Ungodly Will-Power," Originates in the Soul

Evil, then, is an application or exercise of will—by a created, sentient being—that is contrary to the will of God. Therefore, in a very real sense, evil is an intrapsychic force or power; what can be described as "ungodly will-power." Since willing (together with thinking and feeling) is a fundamental and characteristic activity of the soul, evil can be seen to originate in the soul—which is only possessed by an advanced level of sentient being. Moreover, in order to be truly considered evil, a sentient being must *deliberately* and *knowingly* oppose the divine will with their own free-will.

To *unknowingly* oppose the will of God is simply an unfortunate misuse or misapplication of personal will-power; which may be due to a number of reasons, such as ignorance, inexperience, naiveté or incapacity. Nevertheless, even though the misapplication of will may be entirely unintentional and therefore not evil, the perpetrating soul may still reap some undesirable or harmful consequences as a result.

2.4 Minerals, Plants and Animals are Incapable of Evil

From the foregoing, it can be correctly surmised that

minerals and plants are incapable of evil since they do not possess an indwelling soul, nor the capacity of free-will. Even though certain chemical substances can harm or kill a person, it's obviously not the result of evil will-power on the part of the atoms involved. Likewise with plants, some of which can harm or kill a person. Once again, this can't be seen as the evil intention of the plants involved to deliberately oppose the will of God.

In the case of animals, while they certainly possess a rudimentary degree of sentient soul capacity (thereby enabling perception, sensation and feeling), they do not as yet possess ego-awareness and the consequent capacity of free-will. Though animals certainly manifest strong will in their actions, it is an instinctive, innate will-power that cannot be freely and independently applied. A lion, for example, cannot just decide one day to start acting like a zebra; it is compelled by its lion-nature to act entirely according to its innate instinct. Moreover, even though an animal can brutally harm or kill a person, this is obviously not the result of an evil application of animal will-power.

This is not to say that minerals, plants and animals cannot be used for evil purposes by, say, a black-magician. In this case it is the will-power of the black-magician that is evil; the minerals, plants or animals are simply used as a means to manifest the magician's evil will.

2.5 Manifestations and Consequences of Evil, Particularly Sin

Once an evil will is aroused, then any number of thoughts, feelings and actions can be formulated to express and manifest that evil impulse. Whatever the countless manifestations of evil, they will all have one shared consequence (to a greater or lesser degree)—what is known in

Western theology as "sin." Sin is best understood as "the separation from God." This of course makes logical sense: if one is deliberately opposing the will of God, then one is obviously distancing oneself from God. The degree of separation will of course be determined by the degree of evil: terrible and monstrous evil will cause a greater separation from God (sin), than evil that is less serious. Recognizing this spiritual fact, Western theology has differentiated sin into two major categories: (1) mortal sin, and (2) venial sin. "Mortal sin" is so called because the separation from God is of such a serious degree that it threatens the very life of the soul; and consequently, it is more difficult to remedy. Premeditated murder is one such mortal sin. "Venial sin" is so called because the separation from God is not as serious, and therefore it is much more easily remedied.

What Western theology has termed, "original sin," was of such a serious nature in the beginning that it affected every human being. Moreover, original sin continued to afflict all mankind throughout the subsequent ages as an inherited, death-dealing spiritual rupture, until it was finally remedied by the divine intervention of Christ-Jesus.

2.6 The Many Unfortunate Consequences of Sin, Including Hell

All the pain, suffering and unhappiness that human beings experience in the world today can be regarded as the multiple effects of sin; that is, as the numerous consequences of willfully separating from God. If God is correctly understood to be the ultimate source of pure happiness, transcendent peace, unlimited joy, complete perfection, everlasting love, superabundant life, absolute goodness, light-filled wisdom and radiant being, then the more one is separated from God, the more one is separated from all these divine qualities.

The evil consequence that is sin logically results in a decrease and diminishment of these uplifting divine qualities within the soul. The disunited soul, then, depending on the degree of separation, experiences despair instead of happiness, turmoil instead of peace, sorrow instead of joy, deformity instead of perfection, emptiness instead of love, suffering instead of abundant life, foulness instead of goodness, dark and fearful unknowing instead of luminous understanding, and isolated loneliness instead of contented selfhood.

Hell, then, should not be regarded as a horrible place in the universe where God condemns wicked souls to be punished for eternity; but more correctly regarded as a state or condition of soul that is experienced by a sentient being who has willingly chosen to separate from God. The pain, suffering and darkness that the soul experiences in this "hellish" psychic condition is not God's punishment *for* sin; but rather the natural consequence *of* sin, *of* separation from God.

This hellish state of soul-separation only lasts as long as a sentient being chooses to engage in evil. If and when a rebellious being chooses to reunite with God, then their hellish condition will begin to disappear. Theoretically, however, a sentient being can choose to rebel against God for as long as the universe continues to exist. But since the universe is a temporal and finite creation, God can freely dissolve it at any time, and thereby end the condition of hell within it. Therefore, hell cannot last for eternity since only God is eternal. Besides, if hell is the result of separation from God, God cannot separate himself from himself; and therefore hell cannot logically exist within God for eternity.

CHAPTER 3

FAULTY CONCEPTIONS AND THE PURPOSE OF EVIL

3.1 Matter Itself is Not Intrinsically Evil

SOME THEORISTS have simplistically postulated that evil is "the opposite of God." While this assertion certainly contains some truth to it, it is rarely properly understood; and therefore often incorrectly applied. A case in point is the faulty reasoning that often occurs regarding universal matter. According to this argument, if matter is seen to be the polar opposite of spirit, and spirit is understood to be the substance of God—which is good—then matter must be the opposite of good, which is evil.

    The error in this reasoning lies in the esoteric fact that matter is not the antithesis of spirit, but rather a "lower vibration" of spirit. Esoterically speaking, matter is densified or congealed spirit. As such it is a created substance (within the universe) that is finite and temporal; and therefore, limited and coarse when compared to spirit. But being limited and coarse does not make universal matter evil. Moreover, as a lower extension of spirit, matter has a natural tendency to return to spirit, to be eventually drawn back and return to its spiritual origin. Matter, then, does not intrinsically oppose spirit (God); and is, therefore, in no way evil.

This assertion that "matter is evil" was one of the few commonly-held beliefs of the many divergent Gnostic sects[1] that existed shortly before and shortly after the time of Christ-Jesus. Many Gnostic sects also mistakenly viewed the entire universe as the evil creation of an evil being called the Demiurge (or Ialdabaoth). Some even went so far as to equate the evil Demiurge with Yahweh-Elohim.

As with minerals, plants and animals, even though matter itself isn't intrinsically evil, it can certainly be used by wickedly-inclined beings for evil purposes. Furthermore, benign matter can also be debased and corrupted by evil practitioners, both human and supernatural; and thereby transformed into harmful or destructive substances. Even in this case, matter itself is not the source of evil intent, but rather the effect or product of evil.

3.2 Correcting the Faulty Logic Which Concludes that Evil Doesn't Exist

Another popular misconception concerning evil that is based on clever but faulty logic is the notion that evil does not actually exist. This erroneous idea is based on the premise that evil is simply a degree of good; in the same way that dark is simply a degree of light, and cold is simply a degree of heat. By reducing the amount of light energy, a perceived condition called "dark" arises. In this case, light is what exists: dark is simply a small amount of light; and as such, does not exist as a thing-in-itself. Also with cold: by reducing the amount of heat energy, a perceived condition called "cold" arises. In this case, heat is what exists: cold is simply a small amount of heat; and as such, does not exist as a thing-in-itself.

Likewise with evil: by reducing the amount of good, a perceived condition called "evil" arises. In this case, good is what exists: evil is simply a small amount of good; and as such, does not exist as a thing-in-itself. On the surface, this appears to be an intelligent, logical conclusion. There are, however, some faulty assumptions to this line of reasoning which lead to an erroneous conclusion.

Take cold, to begin with. Even though cold is admittedly a designation to indicate a diminished amount of heat, that diminished amount of heat is still a very real, perceptible condition which has a very real physical effect. As proof, simply step out into a freezingly-cold environment without any clothing. It would clearly be a silly and dangerous mistake to stand nakedly exposed and smugly declare that "cold" doesn't exist because it was only a diminished degree of heat. Since it is quite possible to freeze to death from a lack of heat—or cold—then cold obviously has a very definite existence.

Similarly with evil. To deny that evil doesn't exist simply on the basis that it designates a measured amount or diminished degree of something (in this case, good) also speciously ignores the fact that evil has a very real, perceptible effect in the physical and superphysical worlds.

Furthermore, "good and evil" is actually a false dichotomy. The correct opposite of "good" is "bad." Since evil is here understood to be "the willful *opposition* to God," the opposite of evil has to be "the willful *obedience* to God"—what can best be termed, "holiness." To be holy, then, is to freely conform to the will of God and his commandments.

Predictably, in today's secular and materialistic culture, the terms "good" and "bad" can have a variety of non-religious meanings. Esoteric Christianity, however, fully agrees with

Western theology that "truth, beauty and goodness" are transcendental qualities of God's being.[2] Divine goodness can be further understood as the eternal union of divine will and divine wisdom; what constitutes divine, truth-filled activity. Goodness in sentient-beings (whether human or angelic) can best be seen as the degree of "god-ness" that is freely manifested in the soul; that is, the extent to which a sentient being embodies and expresses the transcendent goodness of God's nature.

3.3 Refuting the Misconception that "Good Does Not Exist Without Evil"

An additional misconception that is also based on the false dichotomy of good and evil asserts that "good does not exist without evil." Since evil is seen here as simply a diminished degree along a spectrum of good: if good exists, then evil exists; and likewise, if evil exists, then good exists. This idea is like saying that "light does not exist without darkness," and "heat does not exist without cold."

If good is properly understood as a transcendent quality of God's nature, then of course good can exist without evil since God can exist in himself without evil. Similarly with light and heat; both are identified forms of energy that are not dependent on any reduced degree of radiance (dark or cold) for their existence.

3.4 The Faulty Concept: "Good Can Come From Evil"

Another fallacious precept concerning evil that is often parroted these days in various guises states that "good can come from evil," or that "evil can be used for good," or that "God can turn an evil into a good." It should be obvious at this point that evil is never a good; and that evil can never be a path to good—that is, to the transcendent nature of God. Evil will always cause sin (a distancing from God), and sin will always result in suffering (to a greater or lesser degree). Goodness (or "God-ness) will only occur when evil is opposed, resisted, curtailed, halted, discontinued, overcome or vanquished.

Nevertheless, it is true that by resisting evil, one's moral will-power is strengthened and developed; similar to the way that a physical muscle is strengthened and developed by the resistance of heavy weights. But obviously in this regard, any positive effect that resulted was not directly *caused* by the force of evil, but by *resisting* the force of evil. Human beings (or any other sentient being) will never become good (that is, "God-like") by willfully opposing God (that is, doing evil).

Furthermore, even though the divine nature is omnipotent (that is, all-powerful), God cannot do the illogical; for instance, God cannot make a square circle, or create a second God. In this case, not even God can make a "good evil," or more correctly, a "holy evil." However, God can certainly inspire powerful agents of good within the cosmos to combat overwhelming evil. Such was certainly the case with the incarnation of Christ-Jesus to overcome the evil consequence of original sin. But it would be quite incorrect, then, to regard Christ-Jesus as the good consequence of primordial evil.

3.5 Are Disasters Such as Tornadoes, Hurricanes, Earthquakes and Floods "Natural Evils"?

It is still quite common today to hear environmental disasters such as tornadoes, hurricanes, earthquakes and floods described as "natural evils" or "acts of God." Since the elemental forces of earth, water, wind and fire do not possess an indwelling soul or an independent free-will, they obviously can't intentionally oppose the will of God, and thereby commit evil. Therefore, environmental disasters or catastrophes could not possibly have been caused by some "evil forces of nature." No doubt the term, "natural evil," stems from the non-religious definition of evil, which basically states that "evil is anything that causes harm or destruction to human beings or their property." Other familiar applications of this diluted definition of evil that are commonly heard today are "the evil of cancer," or "the evil of drug addiction," or "the evil of poverty," or "the evil of money," or "the evil of war."

The likewise erroneous notion that natural disasters and catastrophes are "acts of God" is clearly an Old Testament-style perception of God: that he wrathfully inflicts natural disasters on mankind as dire punishment for serious sin. As was previously discussed in Chapter subsection 2.6, an all-loving God does not punish mankind for sin. The pain and suffering caused by sin is simply the natural consequence of separation from God. Once again, we are chastened and bruised *by* our sin, not punished by God *for* our sin.

Nevertheless, as will be discussed in more detail in Chapter 3, natural forces can unfortunately be used by powerful, supernatural beings to physically manifest their evil will-intentions. Moreover, according to spiritual science there is a deep and mysterious connection between the subconscious human will and the subterranean forces of nature; such that the collective force of evil human will-power can actually arouse the fiery volcanic forces beneath the surface of the earth. The destructive power of certain natural disasters, then, may indeed be the result of evil; but that evil was not caused by the natural forces themselves, but by human and superhuman beings.

3.6 The Erroneous Conception that "Free-Will Cannot

Exist Without Evil"

Even though there are many perplexing questions regarding evil, "Why does God allows evil to exist?" is—to the surprise of many—not one of them. Clearly the universe was conceived into existence in order that the Supreme Being could evolve creatures (created beings) in his image and likeness.[3] Even though God cannot logically create another infinite and eternal being (another God), he can create finite and temporal replicas (images and likenesses) of himself. But in order that these created beings not simply exist as living automatons that are blindly dependent on divine control, he needed to grant them the capacity of free-will. This is somewhat analogous to a loving parent allowing their growing child to ignore or disregard their wise instruction, so that the child can experience their own fledgling freedom and independence.

Free-will in a universal sense means the innate capacity or the personal potential of a created being to obey God or to disobey God. To act contrary to the will of God and his commandments (intentions) is, however, what is here understood as evil. In order to enable free-will in created beings, then, God needed to permit "the possibility of evil." It should be clear from the simple analogy used above that it isn't strictly necessary *to act* contrary to the will of the parent for the child to know personal freedom and independence. It is sufficient that the *possibility* exists; that is, it is enough for the child to know that a free and independent action (which is contrary to the parent) *can* be taken if they chose to do so.

Evil is certainly an exercise of free-will, and is definitely not possible without it. However, choosing to obey the will of God can also be an exercise of free-will. Even though evil is possible; that is, even though one can choose to rebel against God, with free-will one can also happily choose not to. In other words, though evil cannot exist without free-will;

free-will can certainly exist without evil. This is especially true in God's case; his omnipotent will is perfectly free without any necessity for evil.

It is also important to note and understand, that even though God has allowed created beings to oppose his will (to do evil), he cannot logically do so himself. In other words, though God allows for the possibility of evil in the universe, his own divine nature is completely contrary and opposed to evil.

3.7 The Faulty Concept: "Without Evil There is No Freedom"

In a broader universal context, then, it is vitally important to realize that it is not necessary to manifestly oppose the will of God in order to be free. Phrased more succinctly: evil does not lead to freedom.[4] As has been repeatedly emphasized, evil always leads to sin, which in turn causes degrees of impairment in body and soul. By willfully separating from God through evil, one becomes bound by (not free from) affliction, suffering, illness, disease and misery. Moreover, since God is perfectly free, true freedom for sentient-beings created in his image and likeness obviously comes from obeying the divine will (and becoming more god-like), not from disobeying it (and becoming more ungodly).

It seems somewhat paradoxical at first that complete freedom for created beings derives from willing obedience to the Creator. The key to solving this apparent paradox is by understanding that obedience to God can be freely chosen, and not forced, necessitated or coerced in any way by God. It is clear from the broad extent of evil in the world that almighty God does not force created beings to blindly obey him. God does not directly override the free-will granted to human and all other sentient-beings in the universe.

Freely obeying the will of God is also encouraged by the realization that the deepest, inmost aspirations of the soul are identical to the ultimate intentions of God. In other words, obedience to the will of God is not a sacrifice or surrender of one's independence of will, but instead the transcendent union and expansion of one's limited will with the omnipotent will of God. True freedom arises when the created soul experiences its own will conjoined with the will of God as one and the same.

CHAPTER 4

SUPERNATURAL PERPETRATORS OF EVIL: LUCIFER

4.1 Know Your Enemy

IF YOU KNOW the enemy and know yourself, you need not fear the result of a hundred battles. If you know yourself but not the enemy, for every victory gained you will also suffer a defeat. If you know neither the enemy nor yourself, you will succumb in every battle.

—Sun Tzu (544 BC–496 BC): *The Art of War*

When one is able to peel back the veneer of physical sense perception and tentatively gaze into the superphysical world that surrounds us all, what becomes frighteningly visible is that a fierce and powerful spiritual battle is raging throughout the vast cosmos. Moreover, from every direction of the zodiac this fearful conflict has penetrated and embroiled the body and soul of every human being.

This intense cosmic conflict is essentially a clash of wills involving the entire range of supernatural beings from angel to seraphim. Arrayed on one side are those beings who are actively united with the beneficent will of God as it manifests in creation, and those beings who are actively opposed to the divine will in the universe. This conflict, then, is battle of holiness versus evil, with two highly-prized jewels going to the victor—the human soul and the evolution of the earth.

Human beings, then, are not just passive spectators in this cosmic conflict; but whether they like it or not, they're at the very centre of this battle. They are in fact one of the cherished prizes, one of the highly-treasured "spoils of war." Whether consciously recognized or not, the unfortunate reality is that every human soul (living and deceased) has been drawn into this conflict—on one side or the other. In other words, whether they realize it or not, human beings are working towards their own soul-salvation on the side of holiness, or they're working towards their own soul-destruction on the side of evil.

What is taking place in our time, then, is a further "war in heaven" that has spilled over onto the earth, and into human souls and bodies. In consequence, the present day is an unavoidable time of moral reckoning—does one enlist on the side of holiness, or does one enlist on the side of evil?

If one freely and knowingly decides to enlist with the cosmic company of holiness to fight for the salvation of the soul and the divinely-destined evolution of the earth, then one must thoroughly, carefully and wisely prepare for battle. As quoted on the previous page by the ancient Chinese philosopher and military strategist, Sun Tzu, one of the most important preparations for victory in war is to "know your enemy"; that is, to know the strengths, weaknesses, intelligence, intentions, alliances, history and strategy of your opponent.

With this in mind, we'll proceed to examine the foremost

proponents of supernatural evil—the principal enemies of human destiny and earth evolution.

4.2 Lucifer: Mankind's Initial Encounter with Evil

As the biblical account in Genesis accurately indicates, mankind's initial encounter with evil was with the seductive serpent in the paradisal garden of Eden. Since primordial human history is conveyed figuratively and allegorically in the Genesis account, the supersensible (clairvoyant) research of anthroposophical spiritual science will be necessary in order to better arrive at more precise and detailed information.

For instance, the Genesis account is poetically vague as to the historical time, location and description of the "garden of Eden." Spiritual science, however, indicates that Eden existed as a superphysical condition about 4.5 billion years ago during what is esoterically termed the Lemurian Age, and geologically termed Hadean time. The earth at that time was in a seeringly-hot, fluidly-molten, magmatic condition which existed before the beginning of crustal cooling and land-mass formation.

Naturally at that time, no familiar life-forms existed on the surface of the Lemurian earth. Nevertheless, invisibly hovering high above the inhospitable surface were ethereal, animal-like human forms that were under the evolutionary direction of highly-advanced superphysical beings.[5] Over extensively-long periods of evolutionary time, the crude human *forms* were refined enough to accommodate an independent immortal soul which enabled the first faint glow of an individualized ego-self—thereby becoming true human *beings*.[6]

Together with the gift of an immortal soul and a vague external sense of self, nascent Lemurian humanity was also granted the emergent capacity of free-will. Prior to becoming human beings, the soul-less human life-forms were under the complete direction of higher beings (somewhat similar to the instinctual direction of today's animals). Echoing the allegorical Genesis account, it was only after acquiring an individualized soul with the capacity of free-will, and then the bodily separation into two distinct genders, that nascent humanity first encountered evil.

This initial evil encounter began as a subtle, covert infiltration of the astral bodies[7] of a few Lemurian human beings, particularly women. Since imaginative forces are more easily aroused in the astral substance of women, the enemy infiltrator began by stimulating false imaginations that were contrary to the truth-filled cosmic images that had been exclusively reflected within the human soul up until then. Since nascent Lemurians, like children today, possessed a strong innate propensity to imitate, they soon began to eagerly generate their own false imaginations. These errant visualizations, in turn, acted as inducements or enticements to inflame the lower passions of the astral body. These unconstrained desires then led to activities that were contrary to positive human development and well-being; that is, they resulted in evil.

The Lemurian inducement to evil was under the direction of a very highly-advanced superphysical being known to spiritual science as Lucifer (Latin: "Light-bearer"). Differing from Western theology, spiritual science does not equate Lucifer with Satan; but recognizes both as very different beings, with very different characteristics and very different evil-agendas.

Though there continues to be an aura of mystery relating to Lucifer's distant past, it appears that he is a retrograde "dominion" or "spirit of wisdom" (please refer to Figure 1 on the following page) who has fallen back to the level of a "virtue" or "spirit of movement." Moreover, at one time he was the planetary spirit of ancient Venus (which today is known as the planet Mercury); but who lost that position after a previous "war in heaven."

	WESTERN THEOLOGY	HEBREW TRADITION	GREEK TRADITION	ANTHROPOSOPHY
THE TRIUNE GOD	THE BLESSED TRINITY (INCLUDES)	YAHWEH	THEOS	THE TRINITY
THE WORD	THE WORD	MEMRA	LOGOS	THE CREATIVE WORD
FIRST HIERARCHY	SERAPHIM	CHAIOTH HA-QADESH	(SERAPHIM)	SPIRITS OF LOVE
	CHERUBIM	AUPHANIM	(CHERUBIM)	SPIRITS OF HARMONY
	THRONES	CHASHMALIM	(THRONES)	SPIRITS OF WILL
SECOND HIERARCHY	DOMINIONS	SERAPHIM	KYRIOTETES	SPIRITS OF WISDOM
	VIRTUES	MALACHIM	DYNAMEIS	SPIRITS OF MOVEMENT
	POWERS	ELOHIM	EXUSIAI	SPIRITS OF FORM
THIRD HIERARCHY	PRINCIPALITIES	BENE ELOHIM	ARCHAI	TIME SPIRITS
	ARCHANGELS	KERUBIM	ARCHANGELOI	SUN SPIRITS
	ANGELS	ISHIM	ANGELOI	MOON SPIRITS
	HUMANITY	BENEI-ADAM	ANTHROPOS	SPIRITS OF FREEDOM

Figure 1: The Universal Hierarchy of Beings

Since the beginning of the present Earth Period, Lucifer has enlisted the assistance of and provided the leadership for a number of rebellious angel-beings who hadn't completed their full development on a previous developmental stage of the earth, known esoterically as the "Ancient Moon Period." These "fallen" angels (also referred to as "Luciferic spirits") were directly involved in the evil astral invasion of unsuspecting humanity during the Lemurian Age.

Allegorically representing Lucifer as a serpent in the Genesis account was not just poetic fancy, but was based on supersensible fact. During the Ancient Moon Period when the present-day angels were undergoing their "human" stage of development, they helped prepare the etheric foundation for the skeletal human head and the attached spinal column. Since the Luciferic angels hadn't entirely completed this etheric development by the beginning of the Earth Period, when they insinuated themselves into the astral bodies of Lemurian humanity, they were clairvoyantly visualized as beings with human heads and long serpentine tails.[8]

4.3 Lucifer's Mistaken Understanding of Freedom

The question naturally arises at this point: "What was Lucifer's motive in corrupting the Lemurian astral body and thereby initiating human evil?" The main underlying reason is that above all, Lucifer cherishes freedom and independence—more than love, power, friendship, adulation or even knowledge. Lucifer, then, is not some power-hungry demon bent on enslavement, control and destruction. Unfortunately, however, he mistakenly understands freedom to include defiance and opposition towards the divine will, and to those obedient celestial beings who strive to realize the will of God in creation. For some unknown reason, even as a "fallen-away" spirit of wisdom, Lucifer has yet to realize that true freedom is only achieved by freely uniting one's own God-given will to that of our loving Creator.

In the case of Lemurian humanity, Lucifer correctly perceived that nascent human beings were still very much under the direction of higher, divinely-inspired beings such as Yahweh-Elohim (the spirit of the moon) and the Solar-Christos (the regent of the sun). At that time, newly-individuated human beings had not really begun to develop their own self-awareness (ego-consciousness), or to exercise their independent free-will. Nascent humanity was like a young child that required loving protection and nurturing in order to properly develop before exercising their freedom and independence.

Lucifer, in his haste, beguiled infant humanity into exercising personal free-will long before humanity was wise and mature enough to understand the consequences. This was analogous to giving young children matches to play with long before they were mature enough to understand and use the fiery consequences. Deliberately inciting the premature use of free-will in order to set mankind "free," therefore, was not an act of benevolence, but clearly an act of evil.

Many esotericists in Theosophy, Freemasonry and even in anthroposophy have regarded Lucifer as a Prometheus-like benefactor[9] to mankind and the instigator of personal freedom. As sentient-beings created in the image and likeness of God, mankind was clearly created for freedom. It's important to realize, therefore, that freedom was divinely-destined to occur, without Luciferic interference, at a divinely-appointed time when mankind was properly prepared. Lucifer merely "jumped the gun," and spoiled the race.

Mankind's premature use of free-will did in fact ignite the fiery passions of the human astral body which, in turn, set the entire world ablaze with sorrow and suffering down through the long, agonizing ages. Even now, humanity is still reaping the consequent pain of Lucifer's "gift of freedom."

Perhaps the best proof that human beings were destined to be free without any interference from Lucifer is Jesus-Immanuel. Even though, as the "heavenly Adam," he was spiritually protected from Luciferic interference in ancient Lemuria, Jesus-Immanuel successfully developed into an entirely-free human being—in fact, becoming the most highly-advanced initiate of all mankind.

4.4 Recognizing Lucifer's Evil Agenda for the Future

Ever since bright Lucifer lost the rulership of his home planet Venus (now Mercury) in a previous war in heaven, he has been consumed with a deep and yearning nostalgia for the past.[10] In all his actions, Lucifer craves for a return to the past—to regain his previous high estate on Venus. Alternatively, he strives to pull the past into the present. Unfortunately, attempting to transfer the present to the past or the past to the present is running contrary to the forward progression of cosmic evolution, and is therefore evil.

Moreover, in lieu of regaining his lost planet of Venus, since the Lemurian Age Lucifer has also been actively working towards fashioning his own independent planet within our present solar system by illicitly siphoning off astral substance from the earth. Furthermore, he intends to populate this anomalous planet with human souls that he has enticed and extricated from the earth. His seductive enticements are "freedom" and "ecstasy"—Luciferic style.

"Freedom," as envisioned in Lucifer's breakaway domain, would be freedom from material existence, gravitational force, physical sense perception and brain-based thinking; together with the freedom to mentally soar into the empyrean heights of the cosmos in order to freely indulge in unrestricted imaginings and creative fancy. "Ecstasy" in

Lucifer's domain would be the perpetual self-pleasure that is derived from continually generating exotically-new, self-indulgent fantasies, visualizations, reveries and imaginings.

Human souls, then, would exist in Lucifer's illicit planetary kingdom as ethereal, angel-like beings who were each held individually suspended in a dreamlike virtual reality of egocentric blissfulness. Fortunately for mankind, Lucifer's plan for the future has so far been thwarted by equally-powerful and divinely-inspired celestial beings.

4.5 Lemurian Humanity's Fall from Paradise

Even though Lucifer has continually laboured to entice mankind away from the material earth, his evil interference during the Lemurian Age resulted in exactly the opposite. The premature arousal of coarse passions and emotions in the astral body caused a corresponding densification of the invisible etheric and physical bodies. As a result, humanity gradually succumbed to the gravitational influence of the earth below, and was slowly pulled downwards to the surface. Esoterically speaking, this is what is meant by the "expulsion from the garden" and the "fall from paradise."

Because of Lucifer's evil intrusion, mankind "fell" into dense materiality; and the invisible physical form (the "phantom"), by attracting the "ashy" material of the earth, became corporeally visible. As related in the poetic language of Genesis:

> So when the woman saw that the tree [of good and evil] was good for food, and that it was a delight to the eyes, and that the tree was to be desired to make one wise, she took of its fruit and ate; and she also gave some to her husband, and he ate. Then the eyes of both were opened, and they knew that they were naked ... (Gen 3:7, 8)

As a result of the fall, mankind became beings of flesh and blood encased in skin. Once again, as related in Genesis:

> And the LORD God made for Adam and for his wife garments of skins, and clothed them. Then the LORD God sent [them] forth from the garden of Eden. (Gen: 3:21, 23)

As Lemurian humanity slowly condensed to the earth, the molten surface correspondingly cooled and cracked into floating landmasses and continental plates. In time the earth's surface was hospitably cool enough to enable Lemurian humanity to live and move upon it.[11] As mankind and its divinely-appointed overseers adjusted the evolutionary plan to accommodate densified physical life on earth, Lucifer and his renegade angelic subordinates continued their evil opposition at every opportunity.

4.6 Lucifer's Love of Self and Overwhelming Pride

A further driving characteristic of Lucifer's nature is his narcissistic, egocentric love of self. Lucifer is infatuated with his own personal self and cares little for the selves of others. In fact, he is so enamored with his own separate being that he continually strives to transform lesser beings—including human beings—into reflections of himself.

Despite his fallen estate as an "unlawful" spirit of movement (or virtue), Lucifer is still advanced enough to remain a being of light (a "light-bearer"). Unfortunately, the supernatural light emanating from Lucifer is entirely suffused with egotistic self-centeredness. This debases the intrinsic beauty of the light into a corrupted facsimile that can best be described as "glamour." The light radiating from Lucifer's countenance is "glamorous," instead of "beautiful."

Moreover, Luciferic light also projects a mesmerizing,

seductive force of attraction that can best be described as "charisma"; which non-verbally says, "Gaze upon the loveliness of my being; wouldn't you love to be like me?" Luciferic love, then, is not a faithful reflection of divine, all-inclusive love; but rather a distorted, selfish imitation of love.

Lucifer's overweening love of self and his glamorous and charismatic demeanor also account for another one of his impelling characteristics—exaggerated pride.[12] In longstanding Christian tradition, it was Lucifer's pride that caused his downfall and expulsion from heaven. In a lecture given on 12 June 1912, as one of a series of lectures published in *Man in the Light of Occultism, Theosophy and Philosophy* (1989), Rudolf Steiner succinctly described the pride of Lucifer:

> Lucifer is a Spirit endowed in his very nature with infinite pride, so great a pride that it can prove a temptation to man. For, as is well-known, there are things which up to a point are not temptations for man but become so when they grow majestic in their proportions, and pride is one of them. When pride is majestically great it tempts man. Lucifer's proud greatness, Lucifer's pride in his majestic figure of light—these contain a seductive element. "Unmanifest light," light that does not shine outwardly but has immense, strong power in itself—that Lucifer has in full measure.

What is rather astounding and baffling for esoteric Christian thinkers to fathom is the idea that Lucifer's pride is so immense that he continues to regard himself as superior to all other beings in the universe; and that before his ignominious expulsion from heaven, Lucifer actually fancied that he himself was almighty God. Since all sentient-beings endowed with self-awareness reflect the personhood of God, it is always a free-will temptation—the closer one advances to God—to erroneously think that one is not a divine reflection anymore, but actually God himself.

4.7 Lucifer's Lemurian Assault on Sensory Perception and Standing Upright

Lemurian humanity, in its earlier animal-like stage of development, was only aware of the external world by means of internally-generated images in the astral body. Soon after the gift of an independent soul and the separation of the sexes, it became necessary to develop the physiological capacity for objective sense perception. With the development of a multi-branching nervous system, the sensory organs were able to be united to a central processing organ, the brain, and thereby provide objective impressions of the external world.

Since the nervous system is physiologically established primarily by the forces of the astral body, and since the Luciferic spirits had some unfinished astral experience in shaping a rudimentary head and spinal column (that is, an etheric central nervous system) during the Ancient Moon Period, they insinuated themselves in its physical formation during the Lemurian Age.

However, had their interfering influence not been arrested by the intervention of benevolent higher beings, particularly the exalted spirit of the sun (the Solar-Christos), the various human sense organs would have taken on a Luciferic, selfish independence. In other words, humanity's sensory organs would be at odds with each other to retain their own particular sense perceptions, and not selflessly transmit and share these perceptions within the soul.

During Lemurian times, it was also necessary for the newly-acquired ego-bearing soul to realign the physical body from a horizontal orientation to a vertical one. By standing upright, the human body was better able to receive the progressive formative forces streaming in from the sun to properly develop the brain; and the progressive formative forces streaming in from the moon to properly develop the newly-acquired reproductive organs.

Once again, Lucifer and his semi-angelic cohorts attempted to interfere in Lemurian humanity's progressive development; in this case, by opposing the upright alignment of the human body. By regressively keeping the human body in a horizontal orientation with the earth's superphysical forces, Lucifer could preserve the dreamy, internal picture-consciousness of animal-like humanity; and thereby more easily enchant his unsuspecting human subjects to live on his "yet-to-be established" renegade planet.

In order to prevent this retrograde, evil occurrence, the illustrious regent of the sun again intervened, and this time fashioned a properly-aligned etheric human form within the earth's astral envelop; which then became the archetypal pattern and catalyst for all other human beings to replicate. If the Solar-Christos had not intervened, then mankind would not have been able to unfold the necessary forces of soul to fully develop self-conscious awareness and the inherent power of free-will. Mankind, then, would never be free; but instead, would have been held spellbound in the past, dreaming existence away in an astral fantasyland.

4.8 Lucifer's Atlantean Assault on the Vital Organs and Speech

According to spiritual science, the Lemurian Age was succeeded by the Atlantean Age, which extended from about 65 million years ago until the last Ice Age (around 10,000 BC). While the earth had cooled considerably by this time, particularly at the poles, it was still hot enough to envelop the planet in thick, steamy fogginess (esoterically termed "fire-mist") which opaqued the sun for millions of years.

Most of Atlantean humanity inhabited a vast continent that was situated where the Atlantic Ocean is today. As the earth's crust continued to cool, the Atlantean continent slowly began to sink beneath the waves, and was further inundated as the atmospheric water vapour condensed and raised the existing ocean levels. Near the end of the Atlantean Age, the atmosphere was clear enough to visibly see the sun and to display previously-unknown solar effects, such as the rainbow.[11] Today, the great continent of Atlantis is completely submerged, and now forms the floor of the Atlantic Ocean.

For much of the Atlantean Age, the human body remained soft and pliable with thick, cartilaginous internal support—rather than a bony skeleton—to maintain an upright position. As the physical body continued to densify and mineralize, the internal organs also needed to adapt and adjust. Once again, Lucifer and his demi-angelic servitors attempted to interfere with this progressive development; and once again, they were thwarted by the benevolent intervention of the higher hierarchies, particularly the sun-spirits and their eminent leader.

If the vital organs had incorporated Luciferic formative forces at that time, they would have discontinued the selfless, harmonious cooperation that was required for the overall health of the body. Instead, each vital organ would have become greedily self-serving and interested only in itself. The lungs would have ceased cooperating with the stomach, and the heart would have selfishly attempted to keep the life-giving blood all to itself. Thankfully, this wasn't to be.

In addition to the "eventually-successful" vital organ adjustment that took place in ancient Atlantean times, the organs that would enable speech expression—particularly the larynx and the brain—were also being physiologically prepared. During the previous Lemurian Age, human beings were entirely speechless, since they could telepathically communicate by exchanging astral picture-images.

Moreover, before speech could occur, it was first

necessary during ancient Lemuria to vertically align the physical body, and then to separate the originally androgynous human form into two distinct genders: male and female. By using only half of their available generative forces for outward reproduction, each gender could then use the remaining generative forces to internally develop the larynx and brain. All this was, of course, done completely subconsciously under the wise direction of the higher hierarchies, particularly the spirits of form (elohim).

Speech development during the prehistoric Atlantean Age was a very long, two-stage process. At both stages of the process, there was unsuccessful Luciferic interference which attempted to usurp the rightful development. Once again, catastrophe in human development was averted by the protective intervention of the Solar-Christos and the benevolent sun-beings.

During the first stage, Atlantean humanity developed the capacity to formulate simple sounds as a means of expressing the inner life of emotion (such as joy, pain, sorrow, distress and happiness); and feelings connected with bodily function (such as hunger, thirst, fatigue, soreness and indigestion). If Luciferic forces had successfully intervened at this stage, then speech sounds would not have been used to openly communicate with others; but only used to primitively vocalize one's own selfish wants and needs entirely for personal satisfaction.

During the second stage, Atlantean humanity developed the basic capacity to use articulated sound to convey impressions and perceptions of the external world. In other words, human beings acquired the rudimentary capacity of using simple words to express and convey images of the natural environment. Atlantean humanity, then, with the benign guidance of higher beings, developed the foundational elements of language for the very first time.

However, this would not have occurred if interfering

Luciferic forces had prevailed. In that event, human beings would still have acquired an ability to use words, but only in a selfish capacity. Each human speaker would independently develop their own set of words. Obviously there would have been no shared communication as we understand it, since each individual would have egotistically developed their own self-contained language.

In developing the physical organs necessary for articulated speech, the three soul-forces of thinking, feeling and willing were actively engaged. For example, in forming and shaping the mouth, the soul-force of willing was primarily involved in formulating the tongue; the soul-force of feeling was primarily involved in formulating the lips; and the soul-force of thinking was primarily involved in formulating the teeth.

The expanded application of soul-forces in Atlantean speech development offered Lucifer and company an opportunity to "liberate" thinking, feeling and willing from their harmonious cooperation together; and set them "free" to independently pursue their own selfish directions. If the Solar-Christos hadn't intervened and prevented this from occurring, then chaos would have prevailed in the human soul as thinking, feeling and willing went their own separate and selfish ways.

4.9 The Physical Incarnation of Lucifer in Ancient China

No doubt, it will come as a huge shock and surprise to conventional Christian believers (and even to some serious esotericists) to learn from spiritual science that, at one time in the past, Lucifer lived as a human being on earth. This highly-significant but little-known event occurred in ancient China around 3000 BC.

In this case, Lucifer didn't incarnate into a human body at

birth; but rather, he indwelt the body and soul of a 40-year-old nobleman who had been educated in the Chinese occult mysteries. It is still esoterically termed an "incarnation," because Lucifer's indwelling ego-forces penetrated, not just the astral and etheric bodies, but as deeply as the physical body of his Chinese host. If Lucifer had merely indwelt the astral body, it would be esoterically termed an "ensoulment."

Through this indwelling incarnation, Lucifer transformed his Chinese host into a highly-influential teacher. In fact, much of the mysterious grandeur and inventiveness of ancient China can be attributed to "Lucifer-in-the-flesh." Moreover, for the first time in human development, superphysical knowledge (that is, the content of the ancient Mysteries) could be grasped by the intellect, and not only received through revelation.

Consequently, the illuminated knowledge that shone from the Lucifer-incarnation quickly radiated throughout the entire ancient world. It is no exaggeration to say that the greatness and sublimity of the ancient pagan mystery-wisdom, including Gnosticism, is directly attributable to Lucifer's Chinese incarnation in 3000 BC. As expressed by Rudolf Steiner in a lecture given on 01 November 1919:

> [T]hrough the millennia directly preceding Christianity, this pagan wisdom was inspired from a place far away in Asia, inspired by a remarkable being who had been incarnated in the distant East in the third millennium before Christ—namely, Lucifer.
>
> [T]here was an actual incarnation of Lucifer in far-off Asia, in the third millennium B.C. And the source of inspiration for much ancient culture was what can only be described as an earthly incarnation of Lucifer in a man of flesh and blood ... The one-sidedness of the gnosis, for all its amazing profundity, stems from the influence that had spread from this Lucifer incarnation over the whole

of the ancient world. (Published in *The Influences of Lucifer and Ahriman*; 1995)

4.10 Lucifer's Attack on Human Thinking During the Graeco-Roman Cultural Era

The various evil interferences in progressive human evolution that Lucifer and his followers have attempted are not, of course, confined to the distant prehistoric past; but have continued into our present day. A further dangerous assailment that was successfully averted by divine intervention occurred more recently during the early centuries of the Graeco-Roman cultural era (which began in 747 BC and continued until AD 1415).

During the height of Greek civilization, mankind was destined to further develop the soul activity of thinking; more specifically, the intellectual ability to conceive and employ clearly-defined concepts and abstract ideas. Since Lucifer has consistently striven throughout the ages to preserve the dreamy picture-consciousness that characterized the Ancient Moon period of earth development, he predictably opposed the evolutionary advancement of clear intellectual thinking.

Many of the wonderful examples of Greek painting, sculpture, architecture, poetry, drama and mythology were inspired by Lucifer in a desperate attempt to enchant the Greek soul away from intellectual thinking, and back into a dreamy fantasy-land of artistic reverie. Needless to say, the development of Greek philosophy and the formulation of logic by Aristotle (384–322 BC) were divinely placed in opposition to Luciferic seduction.

Even so, it took the incarnational indwelling of the exalted Sun-Spirit in Christ-Jesus during Graeco-Roman times to ensure the future spiritualization of intellectual thought, and to prevent abstract thinking from eventually becoming entirely materialistic.

4.11 Assessing Lucifer's Legacy of Evil Interference

The Luciferic assaults on progressive human evolution discussed above are by no means exhaustive or complete. There are countless other lesser assailments that mankind has endured throughout the long ages. Nor has Lucifer changed his evil ways at the present time, or for the foreseeable future.

For those esotericists who continue to regard Lucifer as a great benefactor of humanity, the preceding account should diametrically alter their opinion. It's abundantly clear from spiritual-scientific research that if Lucifer had successfully realized his evil intentions, mankind would in no way be free. Mankind would have continued to exist at a pre-human stage of evolution, without the ability to stand erect, to speak properly, or to intellectually think. In such a condition, existing in a time-warp dreamland of narcissistic self-indulgence on a rogue planet within the solar system, human beings would never have fully developed true self-conscious awareness on the earth, or the divine capacity to love others in true spiritual freedom.

Lucifer did indeed bring initial freedom to human beings, but it was a false and self-centred independence that led to sin—the separation from God and the divinely-created order of the universe. Up to this point in earth history, therefore, Lucifer's evil interference has brought mankind untold misery and pain throughout the ages. Nevertheless, even though he is a determined enemy of holiness in creation, it is crucially important not to turn against him in hate, or disgust, or hostility or resentment. As we've been instructed by our saviour, Christ-Jesus: in order to effectively overcome evil, we must love our enemies—yes, even Lucifer. As biblically expressed:

But I say to you, Love your enemies and pray for those who persecute you, so that you may be sons of your Father who is in heaven; for he makes his sun rise on the evil and on the good, and sends rain on the just and on the unjust ... You, therefore, must be perfect, as your heavenly Father is perfect. (Matt 5:44–48)

It is also important to remember, however, that even though we are required by the decrees of divine love to extend that love to Lucifer as well, we are not to befriend him and thereby dismiss, overlook or disregard his evil activities. At present, even though Lucifer's superplanetary-self continues to abide in the space between Mars and the sun, he has hurled his soul into the sub-earthly abyss. From there he continues to influence human culture through the forces of gold and electricity—both of which he has precipitated and densified from solar and planetary light ether..

Even if our prayers for Lucifer's conversion are answered sometime in the distant future—at a time when he will discontinue his evil ways and befriend the leader of the sun—he will still have an enormous karmic debt owed to humanity that will need to be repaid and redeemed.[13]

CHAPTER 5

SUPERNATURAL PERPETRATORS OF EVIL: AHRIMAN

5.1 Ahriman: Mankind's Second Encounter with Evil

MANKIND'S SECOND encounter with a powerful supernatural being who has been staunchly opposed to progressive human development and to the divinely-fashioned order of the cosmos occurred during the prehistoric Atlantean Age. This being is esoterically known as "Ahriman," taken from the ancient Zoroastrian spirit of darkness, destruction and death.

In familiar Christian tradition, Ahriman is also known as Satan, Mephistopheles and the Devil. These names are usually avoided in spiritual science since they're often associated with all sorts of misconceptions and misinformation. At the same time, however, they can also reveal some colourfully-intuitive folk-wisdom that can be quite esoterically helpful (as will be mentioned throughout this chapter).

It certainly wasn't intended by the spiritual leaders of earth evolution that nascent humanity should encounter Ahriman during its early stages of development. In esoteric fact, Lucifer had also not intended for this particular encounter with evil to occur. The reason why early humanity came under the evil influence of Ahriman was because the astral, etheric and physical bodies became far more densified and materialized than what was intended. Once the physical body began to attract and incorporate lifeless mineral-matter, mankind also began to attract and incorporate the sub-earthly spirit of death—Ahriman.

No doubt, Lucifer doesn't attribute his own evil machinations for this unfortunate turn of events; but instead, he would particularly blame the benevolent sun and moon-spirits. If they hadn't prevented his renegade planet from forming, he could have easily teleported human beings there while they still existed in an ethereal condition, and thereby avoided further material densification. Unfortunately for Lucifer, his faulty reasoning does not change the fact that he was the one who put the evil ball in motion that eventually rolled up to Ahriman's infernal door; nor does it prevent him from amassing a huge karmic debt as a consequence.

5.2 Understanding Ahriman, the "Unlawful Prince of this World."

As has already been pointed out in connection with Lucifer, spiritual science does not equate Ahriman/Satan with Lucifer. Both are well-known to be entirely different beings. In fact, in many ways Ahriman is the antithesis of Lucifer. To begin with, Lucifer is a spirit-being of light, whereas Ahriman is a spirit-being of darkness (more polarities will be considered later).

In popular Christian folklore, Satan is often depicted as the Devil: a satyr-like figure with the horns, beard and legs of a goat. This image is not entirely fanciful; and in some ways, accurately applies to Ahriman. Since Ahriman's own etheric body is desiccated and withered, he lacks sufficient formative force to properly give shape to the lower part of the human form. As Rudolf Steiner has indicated in a lecture given on 20 November 1914 and published in *The Balance in the World and Man: Lucifer and Ahriman* (1977):

> Ahriman will assume the form which indicates a lack of power in the ether-body. It unfolds insufficient etheric force for properly developed feet and will produce hornlike feet, goat's feet.
>
> *Mephistopheles* is Ahriman. There is good reason, as I have just indicated, for portraying him with the feet of a goat. Myths and legends are full of meaning: Mephistopheles is very often depicted with horses' hoofs; his feet have dried up and become hoofs ... for by his very nature Mephistopheles-Ahriman lacks the etheric forces necessary to permeate and give shape to the normal physical form of a human being.

As to where Ahriman fits in amongst the celestial hierarchy of beings, he is esoterically considered to be a "fallen-away" spirit of form (power or elohim), who is currently operating at the level of a spirit of personality (principality or archai). As described by Rudolf Steiner in a lecture given on 20 April 1908:

> [A]mong the Original Forces [spirits of personality or archai] who have really no right to be there is that being whom one is right in calling "Satan"—Satan, the "Unlawful Prince of this World" ... The Lawful Prince is one of the "Powers" [elohim], Yahve or Jehovah; the unlawful belongs to the ranks of the Original Forces. He expresses himself by continually bringing confusion into man's relation to the Time-Spirit, by bringing men to

contradict the Epochal Spirit. That is the true nature of the Spirit who is also called the "Spirit of Darkness," or the Unlawful Prince of our Earth, he who claims to be the actual guide and leader of men. (Published in *The Influence of Spiritual Beings upon Man*; 2011)

Ahriman was cast down to earth—together with a subordinate host of evil archangels—by St. Michael the Archai—in a previous battle in heaven. Consequently, Ahriman and company inhabit the debased, lower-devachanic (heavenly) plane; which sub-physically interpenetrates the molten, subterranean levels of the earth closest to the surface. In this fiery domain, Ahriman wields great power over the sub-earthly forces of destruction, including the forces of volcanism and earthquake activity. Ahriman has also harnessed magnetic force by condensing some of the chemical ether within the earth; and he also employs existing earth gravity to further his nefarious intensions.

One of Ahriman's nefarious intentions is the complete control of the earth and all life on it—including unsuspecting human beings. For that reason alone, Ahriman and Lucifer are avowed enemies; even though they have on various occasions united forces for a common, malevolent purpose. Unlike Lucifer, who wants to have nothing to do with the presently-constituted mineralized earth, Ahriman is happy as a clam to exist subterraneanly within the rigid crustal-shell of planet earth. Where Lucifer continually strives to rise above dense materiality and blissfully melt into empyrean space, Ahriman continually strives to reduce elevated spirituality to a material dimension—he strives to forcefully drag heaven and all its beings down to the earth.

Each of the planets in our solar system has an exalted spirit of form as its "planetary-spirit"—an advanced elohim-being whose task it is to oversee the entire evolutionary formation of the planet. All of the planetary-spirits properly administer their global responsibilities from the superphysical sphere of the sun; except for the planetary-spirit of the moon, Yahweh, who operates directly from the sphere of the lunar orb itself. Since Ahriman himself is a "fallen-away" elohim-being, when he was defeated in heaven and exiled to earth, he decided to usurp the position of the rightful planetary-spirit and claim it for himself. The earth, however, already had a "lawfully–assigned" planetary-spirit (known mythologically as Gaia or Terra). Ahriman, then, as a vainglorious and illegitimate self-appointed ruler, is truly the "unlawful" spirit-prince of this world.

5.3 Ahriman's Early Evil Interferences

As previously mentioned, it took millions of years for the physical bodies of human beings to become densely mineralized enough to come under the negative influence of Ahriman. Consequently, for much of human pre-history it was mainly Lucifer and his minions who adversely interfered in the progressive evolution of the earth and humanity. But since the dawn of the Western European cultural era in 1413, Ahriman has rapidly begun to exercise more and more evil influence on humanity and on earth evolution in general.

Back in Atlantean times, Ahriman's initial involvement was basically to pick up whatever "scraps" were left over from Lucifer's evil agenda. If Lucifer was successful in seductively enticing human souls away from the earth to a renegade planet, then Ahriman would lay claim to the soulless human bodies left behind, and the abandoned planet earth. He could then set up his own sub-astral, earthbound kingdom that would be completely devoid of soul and spirit. So when Lucifer was attempting to infuse forces of selfish independence into Atlantean humanity's vital internal organs, organs of speech formation, and the soul forces of thinking, feeling and willing, Ahriman's subsidiary involvement mainly consisted of etherically contracting and densifying the human anatomy involved.

During the Graeco-Roman cultural era, when Lucifer concentrated on entrancing the Greeks with elevating artistic reverie, Ahriman spent most of his energies on the Romans trying to establish a militaristic, empirical state-machine. As further explained by Rudolf Steiner in a lecture given on 24 September 1916:

> In Roman culture, on the other hand, Ahriman's aim was to help Lucifer by shaping the Roman Empire and what followed it in such a way that it would have become a great earthly mechanism for ego-less human beings. In this way he would have been of assistance to Lucifer. Whereas Lucifer's desire was to extract the juice of the lemons for himself, as it were, Ahriman, working in the Roman Empire, set out to thoroughly squeeze the lemons and to create an entirely mechanistic state organization. Thus do Ahriman and Lucifer play into each other's hands. The plan was frustrated by the development in a preeminently egoistic sense in the people of the Roman Empire of the concept of *Civis*, the citizen. Human egoism, be it remembered, can only develop in physical existence on the earth. Thereby Ahriman's plan to make men into ego-less beings was frustrated. It was precisely the bleakness, the lack of fantasy in Roman culture, the egoism in Roman politics and system of rights that thwarted Ahriman's plan. (This lecture was entitled "Atlantean Impulses in the Mexican Mysteries. The Problem of Natural Urges and Impulses, the Problem of Death" and published in *Inner Impulses of Human Evolution: The Mexican Mysteries and the Knights Templar*, 1984)

It's unfortunately clear, that if Ahriman and his fellow spirits of death were left entirely unopposed, they would eventually solidify everything on planet earth, including human beings. The entire planet would become permanently frozen into a global, Victorian-style, outdoor museum where every life-form would be dried, pressed, preserved, mummified, desiccated, embalmed and entombed. No doubt, Ahriman would proudly regard the entire lifeless wasteland of the earth as a prime trophy of war, and a prized badge of accomplishment on his coldhearted chest.[14]

5.4 Ahriman's Increasing Evil Influence in the Modern Era

If mankind's pagan, pre-Christian past can be termed "the age of Luciferic evil," then mankind's Christian evolutionary period—particularly the "modern era" from the Renaissance to the present—can best be termed "the beginning age of Ahrimanic evil." Whereas Lucifer has had millions of years to insinuate himself into human affairs, Ahriman has managed to virally infect[15] every aspect of modern life in a very short period of time.

With the pervasive contagion of scientific materialism, Ahriman has managed to effectively abolish any notion of soul and spirit from many modern minds. With scientific empiricism—that is, the exclusive reliance on the five physical senses to observe the universe—Ahriman has pulled a curtain of sensory illusion over the eyes of modern mankind.

One very rapidly-effective ideology that Ahriman has devised in order to abolish the notion of spirit from modern thinking is Darwin's theory of biological evolution. This materialistic theory gained widespread scientific popularity and acceptance soon after English naturalist Charles Darwin (1809–1882) published *On the Origin of Species* in 1859. The theory makes the materialist assumption that human beings are simply a species of animal (and therefore devoid of soul and spirit). Moreover, any positive evolutionary change is postulated to be entirely the result of random genetic mutation and blind "natural selection" (or species survivability). Darwinian theory, then, rejects any notion of intelligent design (by God or otherwise) for evolutionary change in living forms. It is disturbingly astounding how modern minds have been spiritually paralyzed and blinded by this Ahrimanic ideology.

Even though Darwinian theory has done a frighteningly-effective job of abolishing the reality of soul and spirit from modern minds, it was only the ideological foundation for an even more annihilating worldview that would quickly arise from the sciences of particle physics and cosmology. At least with the science of biology, there is still a recognition of the forces and processes of life. With modern particle physics and cosmology, however, only the lifeless interaction of atomic particles throughout the universe is scientifically considered.

According to modern-day particle physics and cosmology, the entire universe is dead and lifeless, without consciousness, morality, purpose, intelligence, soul, spirituality or being. What appears to be biological life on earth is scientifically considered to be nothing more than random aggregations of complex molecules. What appears to be thinking, feeling and willing in "human" bodily configurations is regarded as nothing more than purposeless chemical and electrical activity. In the space of a meager six hundred years, Ahriman has managed to convince a great many modern thinkers that the entire universe is nothing more than a gigantic, atomic mechanism; and that human beings are nothing more than chemically-driven man-machines.

Also in connection with this worldview of death and mechanization, Ahriman and his evil entourage have managed to stimulate the development of—and incorporate themselves into—most modern-day machine technology. A great many mechanized inventions today have harnessed forces of destruction in order to operate. An automobile engine, for example, derives mobility-power by harnessing a carefully-contained series of small gasoline explosions. Needless to say, fiery explosions, no matter how small, open the sub-physical door to Ahrimanic infiltration.

The development of automatons, robotics and artificial machine-intelligence—that is, the development of soulless, mechanical humanoid-forms—very much plays into Ahriman's materialistic, long-term plans. By designing machines that are more human-like, it's a whole lot easier to subvert humanity into becoming more machine-like; and thereby sabotage progressive human evolution. Moreover, soulless Ahrimanic beings are magnetically drawn to sub-physically inhabit the lifeless shells of man-made machinery. For this reason, Ahriman is also esoterically known as Mephistopheles—the "god in the machine." By being in close proximity to unsuspecting human beings, Ahriman and his malevolent horde have become an intimate but unseen part of everyday modern life.

By continually promoting the atheistic and materialistic worldview that the universe is nothing more than an astronomically-large machine, and by inundating human industry with "necessary" machine-technology, Ahriman has easily convinced many modern thinkers that human society should also be designed like a well-oiled machine, and that human individuals should best be regarded as simply dispensable cogs in the social apparatus.

What has also effectively and rapidly contributed to the Ahrimanic mechanization of human society in modern times is Marxist ideology. Developed by German philosophers Karl Marx (1818–1883) and Friedrich Engels (1820–1895) in the mid-to-late-nineteenth century, Marxism materialistically asserts that *everything* in human history and society has been determined solely by economic forces. Marxist ideology seeks to deny and expel religious and spiritual forces from all social consideration; and thereby establish a worldwide, atheistic worker's utopia.

Godless Marxist ideology not only finds expression in communist regimes, but also in capitalist nations where the "almighty dollar" reigns supreme. In all capitalist countries today, economic activity is inordinately controlled by secretive, centralized banks who print money out of thin air (called "fiat" money). Moreover, nefarious business interests have cleverly established, "the corporation," a legal entity that has many of the rights and privileges of a living person. Unfortunately, corporations are almost always pathological institutions that are entirely consumed with their own greedy self-interest, and directed exclusively by the "profit motive": the drive to make more and more money by any means necessary.[16]

Ahriman's pervasive presence in modern life does not mean that Lucifer is nowhere to be found. On the contrary, Lucifer is still attempting to entice the human soul away from the earth with new and modern means as well. Many current and popular methods of "getting high" are clearly Luciferic enticements: methods such as extreme sports, escapist movies and books, hallucinogenic drugs, computer games, and virtual-reality technology.

Beyond what has been mentioned thus far, it needn't be necessary to go into further detail in order to esoterically acknowledge the pervasive and destructive presence of Ahriman in modern spiritual life.

5.5 The Destined Physical Incarnation of Ahriman

Outside of those who are familiar with the spiritual-scientific research of Rudolf Steiner, few people today are aware that the pervasive penetration and global spread of materialism and atheism in the modern era is Ahriman's advanced preparation for his destined physical incarnation on earth.

In traditional Christian belief, the incarnation of Ahriman is similarly understood as the "birth of the Antichrist"—which has also been equated with Satan, as well as the "great red dragon," and the "beast with seven heads and ten horns" in The Apocalypse of St. John. Though Christian tradition is notably vague concerning the "where," "when," and "how" of Satan's physical appearance on earth, spiritual science is much more detailed and precise.

As to "when," clairvoyant research has determined that Ahriman's incarnation is karmically scheduled to occur three thousand years after the incarnation of Christ-Jesus. Even so, Ahriman is unlawfully attempting to accelerate that date in order to better take humanity by surprise. In opposition to this, the sun-being St. Michael strives to delay Ahriman's incarnation to give mankind more time to prepare. It is esoterically recognized that the earliest possible date for a premature Ahrimanic incarnation would be 1998.[17] There are two main reasons that this date is Ahrimanically propitious: (1) the combined legions of evil always increase their attacks on humanity at the end of a millennium; and (2) Ahriman's more powerful mentor and overseer, Sorath (who will be studied in Chapter 6), escalates his own attacks on humanity every 666 years after the incarnation of Christ-Jesus. The year 1998 is the third 666 year interval after Christ.

As to "where" Ahriman's incarnation will occur, clairvoyant research has determined that the most likely location will be in the West, more specifically in America. There are also two main reasons for this location: (1) America is the surface region most influenced by the subterranean Ahrimanic forces of electromagnetism rising from the centre of the earth; and (2) despite its religious roots, America is the most powerfully-materialistic and powerfully-atheistic nation on earth today.

As to "how" Ahriman will incarnate in order to corrupt

and destroy mankind and world evolution, Rudolf Steiner indicated some very specific details in a lecture given on 15 November 1919:

> When Ahriman incarnates in the West at the appointed time, he would establish a great occult school for the practice of magic arts of the greatest grandeur, and what otherwise can be acquired only by strenuous effort would be poured over humankind.
>
> Lovers of ease who refuse to have anything to do with spiritual science would fall prey to his magic, for by means of these stupendous magic arts he would be able to make great numbers of human beings into seers—but in such a way that the clairvoyance of each individual would be strictly differentiated ... Confusion would prevail and in spite of being made receptive to clairvoyant wisdom, people would inevitably fall into strife on account of the sheer diversity of their visions ... In this way all culture on the earth would fall prey to Ahriman ... the result would be the establishment of Ahriman's kingdom on earth and the overthrow of everything achieved hitherto by human culture; all the disastrous tendencies unconsciously cherished by humankind today would take effect. (Published in *The Influences of Lucifer and Ahriman*; 1995)

The Catholic Church is also very cognizant of the incarnational strategies of the approaching Antichrist, as indicated by Catholic bishop Fulton J. Sheen (1895–1979) in *Communism and the Conscience of the West* (1951):

> The Antichrist will not be so called; otherwise he would have no followers ... he will come disguised as the Great Humanitarian; he will talk peace, prosperity and plenty not as means to lead us to God, but as ends in themselves ... He will tempt Christians with the same three

temptations with which he tempted Christ ... He will have one great secret which he will tell to no one: he will not believe in God. Because his religion will be brotherhood without the fatherhood of God, he will deceive even the elect. He will set up a counterchurch ... It will have all the notes and characteristics of the Church, but in reverse and emptied of its divine content. It will be a mystical body of the Antichrist that will in all externals resemble the mystical body of Christ.

Since Ahriman characteristically corrupts the masculine forces of the will, to clairvoyant perception he always assumes a misshapen male form. When he appears as the Antichrist, then, he will undoubtedly incarnate in a male body as well. Moreover, when incarnating in human bodies, spirit-beings (benign or malefic) do not as a rule inhabit these bodies at birth. It is far more efficient and effective to indwell an adult body that has been specifically prepared by a human disciple.[18]

Historically, this has been the case with the indwelling of Lucifer in the 40-year-old Chinese nobleman around 3000 BC; with the indwelling of Bodhisattva-Maitreya in the adult body of Jesu ben Pandira around 100 BC; and with the indwelling of the Solar-Christos in the 30-year-old Jesus of Nazareth at the turning point of time.

5.6 Ahriman Appearing as the Jewish Messiah and the Christian Parousia

There are of course various Satanic groups and individuals—as well as some secretive occult brotherhoods—throughout the world that welcome an imminent incarnation of Ahriman. Not surprisingly, they are fully prepared to follow him when he appears. But as Bishop Sheen's insightful description of the Antichrist (quoted earlier) pointed out, Ahriman will not appear as the horned Devil with cloven hooves and reeking of sulphurous fumes. Because Ahriman will come in disguise, what is particularly disturbing to prophetically perceive is that a great many naïve Christian and Jewish believers will unknowingly flock to his side as well.

In the case of Judaism, many believers still await the coming of the messiah, who they envision as a powerful human leader who will claim the hereditary throne of King David, and then rebuild the temple in Jerusalem. Furthermore, he is expected to amass a large army in defense of the Jewish people; gather the twelve, lost tribes together to establish Israel as the greatest nation on earth and Judaism as the greatest religion on earth; which will then usher in an extended era of global peace and prosperity. The problem with this particular conception of the messiah is that Christ-Jesus forcefully rejected it as one of the three evil temptations in the Wilderness. He did indeed become the Messiah; but not an earthly messiah, instead a heavenly one. Should any powerful individual with supernatural ability step onto the world stage at some time in the future and claim to be the Jewish messiah, then, he would clearly be opposed to Christ-Jesus; and therefore, the Antichrist.

In the case of Christianity, many fundamentalist Christians (particularly in America) envision the prophesized "second coming of Christ" (also known as the "parousia") *exactly the same* as the Jewish false-messiah. Unfortunately as well, Christian fundamentalists portray the second coming of Christ in worldly materialistic terms, with Christ appearing as an all-powerful earthly-ruler, instead of a heavenly saviour. If in the future, a forcefully-authoritative figure publicly appeared displaying supernatural ability and claiming to be "Christ come again," then he would clearly be the Antichrist as well.

In connection with the danger of fundamentalist

Christians becoming unsuspecting followers of Ahriman, Rudolf Steiner in a lecture given on 27 October 1919 entitled "The Ahrimanic Deception," gave the following warning:

> The real Christ must be sought today through all that can be gained from a spiritual knowledge of the world.
>
> These very people who swear by the Gospel alone and reject every kind of real spiritual knowledge, form the beginning of a flock for Ahriman when he appears in human shape in modern civilization. From these circles, from these members of confessions and sects who repulse the concrete knowledge brought by spiritual endeavor, whole hosts will develop as adherents of Ahriman.

5.7 Has Ahriman's Premature Incarnation in 1998 Been Successfully Averted?

Thankfully, at the time of this writing (2016) there has been no public appearance of any noteworthy individual fitting Ahriman's incarnational description. If Ahriman had physically indwelt his prepared human host sixteen years ago in 1998, then there would clearly be noticeable signs to that effect by now. However, mankind may not be able to give a huge collective sigh of relief quite yet.

Even though it is clear that Ahriman was not able to incarnate in 1998, since that year was still a very propitious time for evil, it could still be used as the birth-date of Ahriman's evilly-inclined human host. If that is the case, and since most spirit-indwellings occur between the ages of thirty and forty, Ahriman could still be planning to incarnate sometime between 2028 and 2038. Only time will tell whether this will occur or not.

CHAPTER 6

SUPERNATURAL PERPETRATORS OF EVIL: SORATH

6.1 Sorath: Mankind's Third Encounter with Evil

WITHOUT THE EVIL influence of Lucifer, mankind would never have encountered Ahriman during earth evolution; and without the combined evil of Lucifer and Ahriman, mankind would definitely have avoided any earthly contact with a third, even more horrific, supernatural perpetrator of evil. Unfortunately, Lucifer's "little white lie" in paradise has brought mankind to the infernal basement door of our solar system's most powerfully-malevolent being, esoterically known as "Sorath."

In fact, according to spiritual-scientific investigation, Sorath doesn't even rightfully belong to our own solar system; but is an evil intruder from a far-different, far-distant and far-ancient cosmic evolution. What brought him here is his evil will-intention to savagely confiscate the entire solar system, and make himself its unchallenged evil-overlord. Consequently, Sorath has maliciously targeted the divinely-appointed overseer of our evolutionary system, the Solar-Christos. Since Sorath is the self-styled, evil antithesis of the Sun-Spirit, he is also esoterically known as the "Sun-Demon." Moreover, in The Apocalypse of St. John, Sorath is also known as the "two-horned Beast that rises from the bottomless pit."

As a consequence of their repeated rebellions against the divine order of the cosmos, Lucifer, Ahriman and their evil legions were expelled from the heavenly regions and cast down to earth. This was of the nature of an expulsion, spiritually analogous to Napoleon being exiled to the Atlantic island of Saint Helena after losing the Battle of Waterloo. In the case of Sorath, however, he is far too cosmically dangerous to simply exile. Soon after he covertly slipped into our own solar system, then, he was surrounded, forcefully apprehended, and then imprisoned within—not exiled to—the lowest subterranean region of the earth—its seething inner core.

In more esoteric terminology, Sorath is cosmically confined to a degenerate and debased region of the higher devachan that is sub-physically consonant with the geological inner core of the earth. It is also important to note that a supernally-elevated level of the higher devachan is also consonant with the geological inner core of the earth.

The matter at the earth's core, which unfortunately Sorath is able to willfully "command," is basically a retrograde, primeval substrate anachronistically left-over from the universe's primordial beginnings. As such, when compared to the lowest form of matter in existence today, the inner-core material of the earth is horribly and frighteningly decayed and degenerated. Clairvoyantly perceived, it is definitely not the compressed ball of super-heated iron-nickel alloy that geologic science imagines it to be.

It's important to note that even though Sorath the sun-demon has been safely incarcerated within the sub-physical confines of the earth, this does not mean that he has not been able to evilly influence the course of human events. Analogous to a powerful Mafia don continuing to conduct mob business from behind the bars of a maximum-security penitentiary, Sorath has been able to use his less-confined evil henchmen to do his odious bidding on earth. In the past, Sorath has relied mainly on Ahriman and his legions to influence humanity and earth evolution. Nowadays he is increasingly using the evil asuras to perniciously corrupt the earth and all its inhabitants.

6.2 Delving into the Evil Nature of the Sun-Demon

If Lucifer's nature could be described in one word, it would be "seductive"; if Ahriman's nature could be described in one word, it would be "sly"; and if Sorath's nature could be described in one word, it would be "cruel." Whereas Lucifer passionately abhors anything physical, including the physical body and physical violence; and whereas Ahriman dispassionately prefers the material realm, as long as he can mechanize the physical body and physical violence so that they are both cold and bloodless; Sorath perversely revels and wallows in physical degradation, including bodily corruption and blood-soaked violence.

For the sensitive spiritual-scientific investigator, then, delving into the evil nature of the Sun-Demon can be a disturbing, gut-wrenching experience. Nevertheless, it is still crucially important to know more about this powerful enemy of God and mankind in order to recognize his evil ways, and to better protect ourselves from them.

For one, Sorath especially targets the natural, healthy, beneficial, and pleasurable forces of human sexuality; and malevolently seeks to debase and corrupt them into sexual perversities. Under Sorath's evil influencing, what should be tender expressions of mutual love, become cruel, violent, selfish and lust-filled depravities and debaucheries. Where there is rape, bondage, torture, sado-masochism, bestiality, fetishism, orgy-ism and deviance—there you will find the lurid visage of Sorath leering in the subsensible background.

Another thoroughly-disturbing characteristic of Sorath is a rapacious and avaricious lust for blood, both human and animal. Sorath can be accurately regarded as a sub-earthly vampire, a real-life "dracul (devil-dragon) of the deep." In Sorath's case, however, it's not the blood-fluid that he insatiably craves, but the etheric effluvia that emits from violently-spilled blood. He is able to regressively pull this especial life-ether to the inner core of the earth, and there compress and corrupt it into nuclear energy. Of course from Sorath's point of view, the more blood that is violently-spilled, the better for his evil designs; hence his historical interest in promoting large-scale wars and wholesale human slaughters.

A further defining characteristic of Sorath is the perverse-pleasure he derives from inflicting pain and suffering on others. Since Sorath has thoroughly distanced himself from the divine love of God, he is incapable of compassionately connecting to other living beings. Without divine love, Sorath is entirely cut off and separated from other beings. As an isolated entity in a self-perceived hostile environment, his only-perceived option is power—power over others. From Sorath's point of view, it's kill or be killed; eat or be eaten; enslave or be enslaved; control or be controlled. Reveling in the suffering of others, then, is Sorath's perverse pleasure of knowing that he is still the "alpha dog," and the foremost "bully on the block."

Though there are other characteristics of Sorath's evil nature that *could* be examined here, only one further characteristic *needs* to be closely considered here—and that is Sorath's megalomaniacal ambition to become the god of the entire universe. Even though Lucifer once proudly proclaimed that he himself was God almighty, after his last unsuccessful rebellion and expulsion from heaven, he has been fairly content to simply dream of becoming the planetary-spirit of a renegade self-established planet within the existing solar system. As for Ahriman, he too appears to be fairly content with the possible hope of becoming the planetary-spirit of a godless and mechanized earth that remains within the solar system. This pragmatic attitude is spiritually analogous to the American Hell's Angels, who are not particularly interested in taking over the US presidency; but instead, are reasonably content to remain as outlaw bikers on the underground fringes of the social order.

In the mysterious case of Sorath, however, over vast aeons of cosmic time he has convinced himself that there is no self-existent, supreme-being who created the universe. Instead, Sorath believes the universe itself to be self-existent; and that in an amoral "dog eat dog" universe, all life-forms fight to become the most powerful being of all—the "god of the universe." As a superplanetary stepping stone on his way to the top of the cosmic heap, Sorath plans on deposing the exalted Sun-spirit from his current position as leader of the solar system, and then despotically taking over control.

Thankfully so far, it's not going very well for Sorath's evil ambitions. Nevertheless, if nothing else, Sorath has clearly demonstrated over vast aeons of time that he is stubbornly committed to his evil ways, and isn't about to give them up or to become discouraged any time soon.

6.3 Sorath: The Two-Horned Beast of Atlantean Black-Magic

There's a mistaken notion among today's esotericists (including anthroposophists), that mankind's initial encounter with Sorath began in the early twentieth century. This faulty opinion stems from startling information given by Rudolf Steiner in a lecture from 20 September 1924, which stated:

> In 1933, dear friends, there would be a possibility for the earth and everything living on it to perish if there did not exist also that other wise arrangement that cannot be calculated ... Before the Etheric Christ can be comprehended by human beings in the right way, humanity must first cope with encountering the Beast who will rise up in 1933. (Published in *The Book of Revelation and the Work of the Priest*; 1998)

Even though Rudolf Steiner accurately predicted mankind's 1933 encounter with Sorath as the evil animus behind the rise of Adolf Hitler and Nazism, unfortunately this was not mankind's first horrific encounter with Sorath.

If we recognize that Sorath is the prime instigator of all forms of black-magic, then we esoterically perceive that the Beast from the abyss has been violently corrupting mankind since Atlantean times. Black-magic is here understood to mean the deliberate misuse of free-will to manipulate the elemental forces of earth, water, air and fire for entirely selfish and harmful reasons.

Even though the ancient continent of Lemuria was destroyed by volcanic eruptions that were inflamed by the misuse of human will, this was not in the manner of black-magic, and therefore Sorath was not involved.[19] Ancestral Lemurians were natural-born magicians; that is, they were born with a powerful will that easily affected the elemental forces of nature around them. There was no need to acquire this magical ability through diabolical training in the Sorathic "black arts."

The first use of black-magic and humanity's initial contact with Sorath occurred during the middle of the Atlantean Age with the Toltecs. The Toltecs were one of seven distinct

Atlantean races, and the ancient ancestors of today's Amerindians. According to Theosophical literature, Sorath was known to the Atlanteans as "Thevetat":

> Thus, under the evil insinuations of their demon, Thevetat, the Atlantis-race became a nation of wicked magicians. In consequence of this, war was declared ... The conflict came to an end by the submersion of the Atlantis ... (H.P. Blavatsky: *Isis Unveiled*; 1972)

The practice of black-magic on Atlantis was continued by a subsequent race known as the Turanians, the ancient ancestors of today's Turkic peoples.

Since post-Lemurian humanity lost the instinctual, inborn ability to magically control the elemental forces of nature, to reacquire this magic for entirely selfish, egotistical reasons required a "pact with the devil"; that is, it required the complete corruption of the magician's soul by the nefarious forces of the Sun-Demon. To learn from Sorath the dark secrets of elemental control, the black-magician had to surrender his soul to Sorath; he or she had to become like Sorath: cruel, vicious, selfish, egocentric, blood-thirsty, and power-hungry.

Consequently, Sorathic training in black-magic throughout history has required horribly-extreme, inhumane and illegal practices: particularly torture, ritual killing and vivisection of both humans and animals. This is a far cry from the juvenile dilettantism of today's New-age style wiccans, neo-pagans, tantrists, Satanists, Luciferians and black-metal musicians who naively worship the "great horned god." As Rudolf Steiner has disturbingly described in a lecture from 02 June 1906 entitled "The Astral World":

> The black magician has the urge to kill, to create a void around him in the astral world because this void affords him a field in which his egoistic desires may disport themselves. He needs the power which he acquires by

taking the vital force of everything that lives, that is to say, by killing it.

That is why the first sentence on the tables of black magic is: "Life must be conquered." For the same reason, in certain schools of black magic the followers are taught the horrible and diabolical practice of gashing living animals with a knife at the precise part of the body which will generate this or that force in the wielder of the knife. From the purely external aspect, there are certain points in common between black magic and vivisection. (Published in *An Esoteric Cosmology*; 2013)

Fortunately for the rest of humanity, the black-magicians on ancient Atlantis could only wield power over the elemental forces of water and air; they had little command over the forces of earth and fire which had previously caused the destruction of the Lemurian continent. Unfortunately, they were also able to misuse the etheric forces of growth, particularly from germinating plant seeds. When beneficially used, these etheric forces could be used to power small airships. When malevolently used, Atlantean black-magicians could generate egoless creatures with deformed and exaggerated bodies to selfishly use as slaves, fighters or playthings.

It was particularly the magical misuse of the powerful elemental forces of water and air—over thousands of years time—that eventually caused the slow breakup of the Atlantean continent, and its complete submergence beneath the sea.[20] Unfortunately for post-Atlantean cultures, the Sorathic practices of black-magic didn't socially disappear along with the physical disappearance of Atlantis. Instead, numerous black-magicians had previously exported their evil practices to remote colonies around the world long before the final sinking of the last continental remnant, around 10,000 BC.

6.4 Sorathic Black-Magic in the Post-Atlantean Age

Sad to say, but no post-Atlantean cultural era has been entirely immune from the corrupting effects of the horrible black-magical practices that derive their power from the two-horned beast from the bottomless pit—Sorath.[21] While numerous examples could therefore be discussed, only two highly-significant ones will be necessary to demonstrate that the evil of Sorath is not a recently-new encounter for humanity.

During the second post-Atlantean cultural era—known as the Ancient Persian—which lasted from 5067 BC until 2907 BC, a fierce battle took place in the Middle East between the ancient Iranians and the ancient Turanians. The historical research of spiritual science has determined that this battle was "the greatest opposition that existed in post-Atlantean civilization ... one of the greatest wars that have ever been fought, of which external history records very little, since it falls in primeval ages."[22]

The ancient Persian-Iranians were mostly descendents of two Atlantean sub-races—the Akkadians and the Original Semites—who had settled in the area now known as Iran. On Atlantis, these peoples had begun to newly develop the early rudiments of intellectual thinking and external sensory perception. Correspondingly, these new acquisitions entailed the gradual loss of the old, instinctive, dreamy clairvoyance that all Atlanteans once possessed.

In contrast, the Turanians of the Ancient Persian cultural era were mostly descendents of the Atlantean Turanians who had migrated to the northern regions of Asia, now known as modern-day Russia and Siberia. These peoples atavistically retained some of the old Atlantean clairvoyance, and continued to practice some of the black-magic that they had powerfully developed on Old Atlantis.

Unlike the ancient East Indians, the ancient Iranians did

not regard the sense-perceptible world as "maya" or illusion; but rather, as an imperfect arena that required divine transformation through human effort. Consequently, the ancient Iranians were an energetic and industrious people who worked to establish a peaceful, agrarian-based, spirit-filled civilization on earth.

By contrast, the ancient Turanians to the north of Iran used their degenerate clairvoyance to parasitically scavenge whatever they selfishly needed off the land. As described by spiritual science:

> At this time ... most of those who were endowed with a clairvoyance that had fallen into decadence, were nomadic peoples, people without a settled dwelling-place, wandering shepherds careless of earthly possessions, and ready to destroy anything if its destruction might serve their needs. Such people were not suited to raise the level of culture, to conserve the gifts of Nature, or cultivate the earth.
>
> The Turanians in the north towards Siberia, who had inherited a lower astral clairvoyance, had no desire to establish external civilization, and their passive disposition, influenced by many priests who practiced magic, led them frequently to occupy themselves with lower magic, and even black magic. To the south, the Iranians, with an inclination to influence the sense-world by their human spiritual force, were working in a primitive way at the beginnings of civilization. (Rudolf Steiner: from a lecture given on 01 September 1910, and published in *According to Matthew: The Gospel of Christ's Humanity*; 2003).

It was karmically inevitable, then, that the progressive Iranians would come into serious conflict with the degenerate Turanians and their Beast-inspired black-magical culture. According to spiritual-scientific research, this little-known prehistoric war on earth fiercely lasted for hundreds of years. It was only through the divinely-inspired teachings of history's first Zarathustra, that the fire-worshipping, Sorath-controlled black-magicians of Turania were successfully repelled and eventually defeated.[23]

A second, little-known (outside of esoteric circles) historical conflict with Sorath-controlled black-magic occurred in the Western Hemisphere during the Graeco-Roman cultural era. After the final submergence of Atlantis, evil descendents of the Toltecs established a powerful centre of black-magic in present-day central Mexico. For centuries there, they unopposedly performed the most heinous practices of Sorathic black-magic; particularly, ritualistic human sacrifice where the heart or stomach would be excised from a living victim.

As a nefarious result, just prior to the birth of Christ-Jesus, there arose in pre-Columbian Mexico the most powerful black-magician the world has ever known. If this demonic human spawn of Sorath had not been vanquished, then instead of European civilization conquering America, it would have been Toltec black-magic sweeping over Europe. Needless to say, the course of human history would have been entirely corrupted and diverted.

Thankfully, an equally-powerful initiate of the Sun-Spirit, known as "Vitzliputzli" in spiritual science,[24] physically vanquished the black-magician, extirpated his etheric memory, and psychically imprisoned his astral vehicle and iniquitous powers. Such extreme measures were necessary in order to prevent future black-magicians from clairvoyantly accessing these prodigious diabolical secrets. According to the clairvoyant research of Rudolf Steiner:

> Then a conflict began between this super-magician and ... Vitzliputzli ... The three year conflict ended when Vitzliputzli was able to have the great magician crucified [at about the same time as Christ], and not only through

the crucifixion to annihilate his body but also to place his soul under a ban, by this means rendering its activities powerless as well as its knowledge. Thus the knowledge assimilated by the great magician of Taotl was killed. (From a lecture given on 01 January 1909 entitled "Mephistopheles and Earthquakes," and published in *The Deed of Christ and the Opposing Spiritual Powers*; 1976)

From the two historical events here delineated, it is disturbingly clear that Sorath the sun-demon is an ancient and formidable enemy of mankind. When the Beast emerged in the twentieth century, he appeared in a new, horrific disguise—German Nazism. Concurrently, Lucifer was the driving force behind Bolshevism in Russia; while Ahriman instilled Fascism in Italy.

As was the case in prehistoric Persia and pre-Christian Mexico, Sorathic black-magic was the occult power behind the scourge of Nazism. In this instance, however, Adolf Hitler and his inner circle of Nazi henchmen didn't need to engage in ritual blood sacrifice in order to acquire black-magical ability;[25] they had already acquired this evil capacity as black-magicians on ancient Atlantis. Thankfully, they had lost the power to command the elemental forces of nature; but unfortunately, they retained the power to hypnotically control large masses of people.

So, as spiritual-scientific research accurately foretold, the Beast from the bottomless pit did indeed begin to "rise up in 1933." But unfortunately, Nazism wasn't the only Sorathic evil during this dark time of the twentieth century that rose up out of the belly of the Beast. When the American military dropped two atom bombs on the Japanese cities of Hiroshima and Nagasaki in 1945, Sorathic power also rose up out of the subterranean depths in the form of degenerate life ether—that is, in the destructive form of nuclear energy.

Fortunately for mankind and earth evolution, the "rising up of the Beast" in the twentieth century does not mean that

Sorath has been released from sub-earthly imprisonment. Nevertheless, mankind's destructive flirtation with black-magic since Atlantean times, and the modern-day development of nuclear weaponry, has gradually weakened the spiritual force-field surrounding the earth that keeps the Beast contained. Consequently, Sorath is better able to rise up into the thoughts, feelings and will-forces of the human soul, in order to bring about its complete and utter annihilation.

Once again, mankind can thank the compassionate intervention of the exalted Sun-Spirit for continued protection from supernatural evil. By continuing to indwell Christ-Jesus until the "end of the age," and by becoming the new planetary-spirit of the earth, the superplanetary Saviour of mankind is slowly transforming our planetary home into a future sun by gradually irradiating the subterranean regions with spiritual light and divine love. In consequence, Sorath will either begin to embrace the light by renouncing his evil ways, or he will choose to retreat ever deeper into the darkness of his own being. In either case, there will come a future time when Sorath is no longer a destructive threat to human advancement.

6.5 Sorath and the Infernal Circle of Twelve

Since demonic spirits and black-magicians intentionally distance themselves from God—the "divine creator"—they are characteristically "uncreative." True creative power only derives from the will and wisdom of God. Consequently, demonic spirits and black-magicians don't create; they can only destroy. In other words, their entire nefarious activity is simple; they take whatever is god-like or divinely-inspired, and do the opposite: reverse it, invert it, corrupt it, defile it or destroy it. If something is the truth, they will turn it into a lie. If something is beautiful, they will strive to make it ugly. If something is good, they will do whatever they can to make it bad.

This is not to say that practitioners of evil—both human and superhuman—don't *appear* to be clever, intelligent or inventive. Take Ahriman, for example. As a spirit-being who is far older than humanity, Ahriman has acquired a vast storehouse of knowledge and experience. Very much like a modern computer, he can randomly generate all sorts of new and seemingly-original combinations from pre-programmed information. In Ahriman's case, what comes out is entirely dependent on what has gone in; he has no divine inspiration when it comes to ideas.

Ahriman and his like-minded subordinates have been falsely credited with inspiring many of our modern-day technological inventions; when in fact, all that they have done is clairvoyantly access future inventions, and then materialistically distort them. Ahriman and company will never introduce a new technology or invention that will assist or promote human advancement. They will only take a beneficial invention and corrupt it; after all, their short-term intention is to populate the planet with soulless humanoid creatures—not human beings.

One of the many evil inversions that Sorath has established in the underworld is a shadowy counter-image of Christ-Jesus and the twelve apostles. When our Saviour surrounded himself with twelve apostles, he was merely applying the "universal law of twelve," which basically states that: "In order to completely conceal a sphere in physical space, it must be surrounded by twelve spheres of identical size; likewise, in order to completely understand any idea in mental space, it must be surrounded and perceived from twelve different viewpoints."[26]

Where Christ-Jesus surrounded himself with twelve holy men to fully comprehend his mission, and to comprehensively convey his teachings after his ascension,

Sorath has inversely surrounded himself with twelve evil spirit-beings in order to completely conceal himself from mankind, and to comprehensively attack earthly evolution from twelve different directions. This "infernal circle of twelve" (also known as the "twelve princes of hell") is currently comprised of:

(1) Lucifer: the evil-spirit of selfish wisdom-light
(2) Ahriman: the evil spirit of materialistic darkness
(3) Asmodeus: the demon of lust and revenge
(4) Merigum: the demon of turbulence
(5) Apollyon (Abaddon): the demon of fury and destruction
(6) Astaroth: the demon of defamation and speciousness
(7) Mammon: the demon of greed and temptation
(8) Moloch: the demon of idolatry, and the devourer of children
(9) Nisroch: the demon of hatred, despair and fatality
(10) Lilith: the demon of debauchery and abortion
(11) Adramelek: the demon of murder
(12) Belial: the demon of anarchy

All the demonic leaders fearfully obey Sorath's evil commands without question, except for Lucifer (of course). Since Lucifer embodies egocentric independence, he has agreed to cooperate with Sorath's nefarious plans as long as he remains free to pursue his own selfish designs. In an inversely-analogous way, then, Lucifer is the "Judas" of the group. Moreover, even though Lucifer's lower nature has been exiled to the sub-earthly regions of our planet, his higher nature still occupies the interplanetary space between the sun and Mars.

Ahriman also occupies a unique place in the infernal circle of twelve. Even though Sorath is loathe to share power, he has appointed Ahriman as his "second-in-command," only because he needs Ahriman's proximity to the surface of the earth. Since Sorath continues to be confined to the earth's inner core, in order to attack humanity on the surface—in order to "rise up out of the abyss"—he needs to project his corrupting power through the subterranean mantle region of Ahriman.

6.6 Sorath and the Sub-Surface, Etheric Realm of Agharti

As understood in esoteric Christianity, when Christ-Jesus "ascended into heaven" he took up "seasonal" residency[27] in the light-filled etheric region invisibly surrounding the earth, known as "Shambhala." When abiding in Shambhala, our Saviour is surrounded by twelve human bodhisattvas, who together wisely oversee the progressive evolution of the world.

Not surprisingly, the forces of evil have established a distorted counter-image of Shambhala in the debased etheric region just below the earth's surface. This dark subterranean domain is inhabited primarily by fallen angels and discarnate black-magicians.

As well, there is a centre of concentrated evil that is deliberately situated in the Agharti region immediately below present-day Jerusalem. Known by its biblical name, "Babylon," this centre of Sorathic black-magic is the evil mirror-image of the heart-centre of Shambhala—known biblically as the "New Jerusalem"—which is opposingly situated in the etheric region above present-day Jerusalem.

CHAPTER 7

THE INVERSE TRIAD OF EVIL: LUCIFER, AHRIMAN AND SORATH

7.1 The Great Universal Law of Triplicity

SINCE THE UNIVERSE, in the beginning, was created in the "image and likeness of God," everywhere and everything in creation reflects the trinitarian nature of the divine Creator. Esoteric Christianity fully concurs with conventional Christian theology that the One God is a perfect union of three divine persons; familiarly known as Father, Son and Holy Spirit. Therefore, any image or likeness in the created universe must in some way reflect (to a greater or lesser degree) the three divine persons of God.

Even powerful perpetrators of evil—such as Lucifer, Ahriman and Sorath—cannot escape, undo, oppose or deny "the great universal law of triplicity." To begin to understand exactly how this universal law also applies to evil, it is necessary to gain a much deeper understanding of the divine Trinity, and then discern precisely how the Trinity is reflected in the created universe.

7.2 The Universal Principle of Rhythm: The Forces of Expansion, Contraction and Equilibrium

A good place to start in a sincere effort to gain a better understanding of the divine Trinity is to examine the fundamental workings of the universe; and in this case, using esoteric knowledge wherever possible. One widely-recognized observation of the universe is that everything is in constant motion; and that this incessant motion, in whatever form it takes, is fundamentally rhythmic. Waves of the ocean rise and fall; the sun in the sky comes up and goes down; our respiratory breathing comes in and goes out; in the day we're awake and at night we're asleep; we're hot in the summer and cold in the winter; first we're born and then we die.

This fundamentally-rhythmic characteristic of the physical universe has been esoterically recognized for thousands of years, as indicated in the Hermetic teachings of ancient Egypt and Greece.[28] As stated in *The Kybalion: A Study of the Hermetic Philosophy of Ancient Egypt and Greece* (2013):

> "Everything flows, out and in; everything has its tides; all things rise and fall; the pendulum-swing manifests in everything; the measure of the swing to the right is the measure of the swing to the left; rhythm compensates."—*The Kybalion*.

> This Principle embodies the truth that in everything there is manifested a measured motion, to and fro; a flow and inflow; a swing backward and forward; a pendulum-like movement; a tide-like ebb and flow; a high-tide and low-tide; between the two poles which exist in accordance with the Principle of Polarity ... There is always an action and a reaction; an advance and a retreat; a rising and a

sinking. This is in the affairs of the Universe, suns, worlds, men, animals, mind, energy, and matter. This law is manifest in the creation and destruction of worlds; in the rise and fall of nations; in the life of all things; and finally in the mental states of Man.

The key to understanding the universal principle of rhythm is to recognize that *everything* in the physical universe comes under the sway of three fundamental forces: (1) the force of contraction, (2) the force of expansion, and (3) the force of equilibrium. It is also important to note that these three essential forces *always* operate together; there is *never* one without the other.

The force of contraction is a centripetal activity that pulls inwardly towards a central point; while the force of expansion is a centrifugal activity that pushes outwardly towards a surrounding periphery. Once these two opposing forces are activated, then the force of equilibrium is engaged. Once the force of equilibrium is engaged, then the centripetal and centrifugal forces are brought into a harmonious balance, whereby the force of contraction will equal the force of expansion. Each opposing force, then, will be prevented from dominating the other; or from continuing to a harmful extreme.

In general operation, once the centripetal activity of contraction begins, there is an inward pull towards the centre. This contraction does not continue indefinitely; but only for a designated period of time, due to the force of equilibrium which overcomes the weakened centripetal force and pulls it back to the starting point of contraction. Once back at the starting point, the momentum of return is conjoined with the centrifugal force which causes an outward expansion towards the surrounding periphery. As with the centripetal activity, the centrifugal activity does not continue indefinitely; but is also pulled back to the initial starting point by the force of equilibrium. Once at the initial starting point, the momentum of return is conjoined with the centripetal force, which results in another contraction towards the centre. The continuous back-and-forth, in-and-out alternation between contraction and expansion is what constitutes "rhythm.". The length of time that a rhythmic motion will continue depends on a number of factors; such as the initial strength of contraction, or the nature of the medium (for example, is it solid, liquid or gaseous). Since the three forces of contraction, expansion and equilibrium govern everything in the physical universe from tiny atomic particles to gigantic cosmic nebulae, everything in creation is consequently subject to the universal principle of rhythm.

7.3 The Universal Principle of Vibration

At the foundational level of the physical universe—at the underlying level of matter and energy—the back-and-forth rhythmic oscillations of atomic particles is commonly termed "vibration," and the rapidity of vibration is commonly termed "frequency." Moreover, molecular vibration correspondingly produces rhythmically-pulsating energy waves that have a measurable frequency of vibration as well. It is no exaggeration to say, then, that everything in the physical universe is in vibratory motion.

What we perceive as different states of matter and different kinds of energy are determined by the frequency of vibration. Molecules which constitute a liquid have a higher frequency of vibration than do molecules of a solid. Molecules of plasma have an even higher frequency of vibration than do solid, liquid or gaseous molecules.

In regard to energy, light waves have a much higher frequency of vibration than do sound waves. Moreover, the various sounds and the various colours of these two separate energies are also due to the frequency of vibration. In listening experience, the higher the musical note, the higher the sound vibration. In visual experience, the colour blue has a higher vibrational frequency than the colour red.

This fundamental vibratory characteristic of the physical universe (fully acknowledged by modern science) has also been esoterically recognized for thousands of years, as once again indicated in the age-old Hermetic teachings:

> "Nothing rests; everything moves; everything vibrates."—*The Kybalion.*
>
> This Principle embodies the truth that "everything is in motion"; "everything vibrates"; "nothing is at rest"; facts which Modern Science endorses, and which each new scientific discovery tends to verify. And yet this Hermetic Principle was enunciated thousands of years ago, by the Masters of Ancient Egypt. (Ibid.)

7.4 The Cosmic Manifestation of Universal Mind

Since modern-day materialistic (empirical) science only recognizes the sense-perceptible universe, it concentrates exclusively on physical matter and energy. Consequently, when dealing with vibration, it is only concerned with the vibratory activity of matter and energy. Due mainly to the relativity theories of Albert Einstein (1879–1955), physical science currently acknowledges that matter and energy are interconvertible; and that matter is a lower vibratory form of energy, and that energy is a higher vibratory form of matter.

Esoteric researchers, however, have recognized since ancient times that energy, itself, is a lower vibratory form of another "higher-something." That higher-something has been variously referred to as "mind," or "mental material," or "noetic essence" or "logoic substance." Whatever the designation, this higher form of energy is esoterically understood to be the underlying substrate to the entire universe. Moreover, it is best characterized as "intelligent energy" that is suffused with life, consciousness, morality and purpose. As explained in Yoga philosophy:

> The Yogis teach that this *Chitta* or Mind-substance, is universal and omnipresent—that is, exists everywhere, and is found at every place in the Universe. Its sum-total is fixed and cannot be added to or taken away from, and therefore it is unchangeable in its sum-total, although like Matter and Energy many apparent changes may occur within itself, resulting from the forming of new combinations.
> Mind-substance may be considered as a higher phase of Energy or Matter, just as Matter may be considered as a grosser form of Mind-substance or Energy. (Yogi Ramacharaka: *Advanced Course in Yogi Philosophy and Oriental Occultism*; 2006)

As with matter and energy, there are numerous states of universal mind, from very coarse to super-refined, that are determined by the degree of vibration. All the separate minds possessed by all the various life-forms and beings in creation, are derived from the vast ocean of universal mind. Moreover, the universal principle of rhythm manifests in all forms and degrees of universal mind as well. However, the ubiquitous forces of contraction, expansion and equilibrium take on a much more personalized and vital character on the vibratory level of universal mind. At the mental level of the universe, what manifests in the physical world as the centripetal force of contraction is here better understood as the "universal masculine principle." Likewise, what manifests in the physical world as the centrifugal force of expansion is here better understood as the "universal feminine principle." And what is referred to as the force of equilibrium is here better understood as the "principle of universal harmony."

In other words, what manifests at a lower vibratory level as the basic mechanical forces of contraction and expansion, at a higher vibratory level operate as a vitalized, gendered interaction of masculine and feminine principles. Likewise, since the principle of universal harmony "springs" from the interaction of the masculine and feminine principles, it is accurately considered to be the "mental offspring," or the "mental progeny" of these two principles.

To illustrate the characteristic difference between the physical and mental worlds, take the basic formation of a typical sub-atomic particle (as esoterically envisioned). When there is an elemental contraction in etheric space, a rarefaction occurs; that is, a tiny hole in etheric space is opened up. As the chemical ether is drawn in, a spinning vortex begins to form around the initial point of collapse. As more chemical ether is drawn in, the rotational movement of the vortex accelerates and the hole gets smaller and smaller.

When the rotational acceleration of the vortex reaches a certain speed (the point of equilibrium), the centrifugal force of expansion is activated, and the rotating ether begins to be forced outwardly. Once this occurs, the hole in etheric space begins to widen. As the hole widens, more ether is drawn in, further accelerating the speed of rotation and the outward expansion.

This outward expansion eventually causes a peripheral compression or densification of etheric space around the rapidly-spinning vortex (this is what science calls the "mass" of a sub-atomic particle). This compression arrests the outward expansion of centrifugal force, and causes the compressed ether to rebound back into the initial rarified opening of the vortex. Once this occurs the entire process of contracting and expanding, of rarefaction and compression, repeats itself again and again. Since ether is essentially frictionless, the rhythmic, in-and-out oscillation of a sub-atomic particle will continue for a very long time, unless there is some interference by a stronger force. The resulting particle looks very much like a rotating toroidal vortex, as illustrated in Figure 2 below.

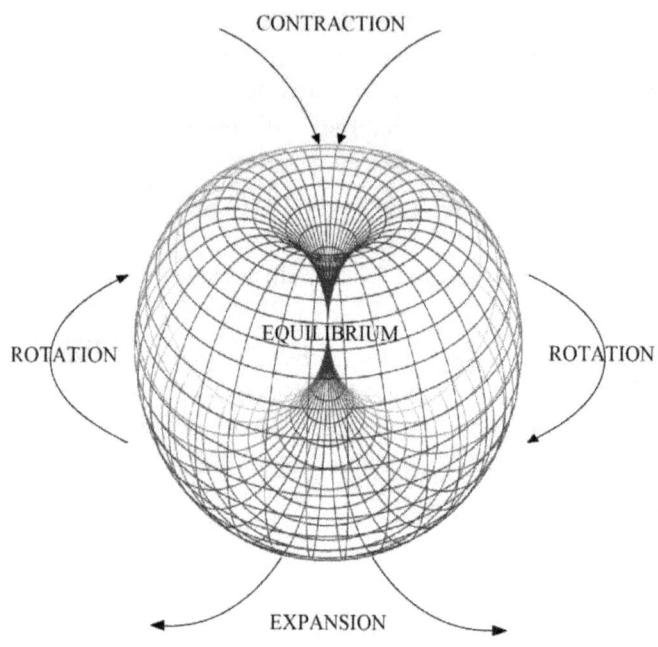

Figure 2: Basic Diagram of Generic Sub-Atomic Particle

Correspondingly within the universal mind, when the masculine principle is engaged and a contraction of mental space begins, a temporary vacuum in mental space opens up. As mental space is increasingly drawn towards the centre, a spinning vortex occurs around the mental opening. At the point of harmonious balance, a bright point of illumination occurs at the centre (called an "idea"). Together with accelerating vortex rotation, the point of intense mental illumination ignites the feminine principle to radiate this mental illumination outwardly in all directions, to the point where it compresses the surrounding mental space. At this point the seed-idea is "firm" enough to be called a "thought."[29] Once the feminine principle has lost outward momentum, the principle of harmony and balance draws the diffuse mental material back to the initial mental opening; where it is once again taken up by the contractive force of the masculine principle, which continues the rhythmic, back-and-forth alternation. Similar to sub-atomic particles, once a thought is formed in ephemeral mental space it can vibrationally endure for long ages of time.

At the level of universal mind, the masculine and feminine principles are generative forces that are both required in order to "conceive" a thought. The masculine principle provides the initiating seed-idea. The feminine principle takes this seed-idea, then expands and develops it into a usable thought. The principle of harmony maintains an equal balance between the masculine and feminine principles, thereby ensuring that neither principle over-reaches to an unhealthy extreme.

What is important to know at this point, is that the universal mind, together with the rhythmic activity of the universal masculine principle, the universal feminine principle and the principle of universal harmony are all lower vibrations of an even higher "something."

7.5 Universal Mind as a Lower Vibration of Universal Being

As has been secretly understood by esotericists for thousands of years, universal mind, energy and matter are all lower vibratory manifestations of a still higher vibration of universal mind. This higher level of universal mind is characteristically more alive, with an innate sense of being and self-awareness. In other words, at the highest vibratory level of creation, the universe is in very truth a living, actualized universal being. In various esoteric traditions this universal being has come to be known as the Primal Man, as the First Adam, as Adam Kadmon, as Purusha, as Hiranyagarbha, as the World Soul, as Anthropos, as the Logos, as the Cosmic Word, and as the Great "I AM." Whatever the given name, the esoteric understanding remains the same: the universe is not a lifeless, insensate chemical corpse of matter and energy, but is instead a fully-conscious universal being.

Within this universal being are all the other countless life-forms and lesser beings that co-exist on various vibratory levels of matter, energy and mind. Nevertheless, for all his macrocosmic magnificence, the universal being had a beginning; and is therefore, the awesome effect of a still more ineffable higher cause.

7.6 Universal Being as a Lower Vibration of Spirit

Since the higher cause that brought the universal being into existence far transcends the workings of the universal mind, it is difficult to form mental conceptions about it. Nevertheless, even though it is challenging to mentally comprehend what exactly that higher cause is, even the ordinary human mind has the ability to detect the presence of this "higher something," and to confidently know that it transcendently exists. The name that is traditionally and commonly given to the "higher cause" of the universe is "spirit."[30]

Since the universal being is a lower vibratory manifestation of spirit, it can also be correctly regarded as a creation of spirit. Moreover, even though spirit can be correctly understood as a much higher form of universal mind and being, it is substantially different in *two* important respects. As a spirit-creation, universal mind and being are finite and temporal; as the creator of universal mind and being, however, spirit is *infinite* and *eternal.* Spirit, then, can be somewhat understood as "infinite and eternal mind-being"; and the universal being can be alternatively understood as "spiritualized universal mind" (for a diagrammatic representation of the various vibratory levels, please refer to Figure 3 on the following page).

In a far-transcendent manner, the spirit creation of universal being can be understood as a "conception" within the infinite and eternal mind-being of spirit. In fact, as the initial lowering of spirit vibration, universal being is the highest conception of spirit mind-being. When spirit mentally reflects upon itself, universal being is conceived in reality. Universal being, then, can also be understood as the highest reflection of spirit. Since spirit is reflected in universal being, esoteric investigators can acquire addition knowledge of transcendent spirit by examining its reflection within the universal being.

Even though spirit is most accurately and most fully reflected at the highest vibratory level of universal being, it is also decreasingly reflected within the three great manifestations of universal being: universal mind, universal energy and universal matter.

At the higher levels of the human mind, spirit reveals itself to be real and unchanging; in fact, it is reality itself, and the source of all reality within the universe. As well, spirit reveals itself to be fully alive, and the source of all life in the universe. Spirit is also perceived to be essentially pure-being, all-knowing, all-powerful and all-loving. In other words, spirit is what we have come to refer to as "the Absolute," or "the One," or "the All," or "the Supreme Being"—or "God."

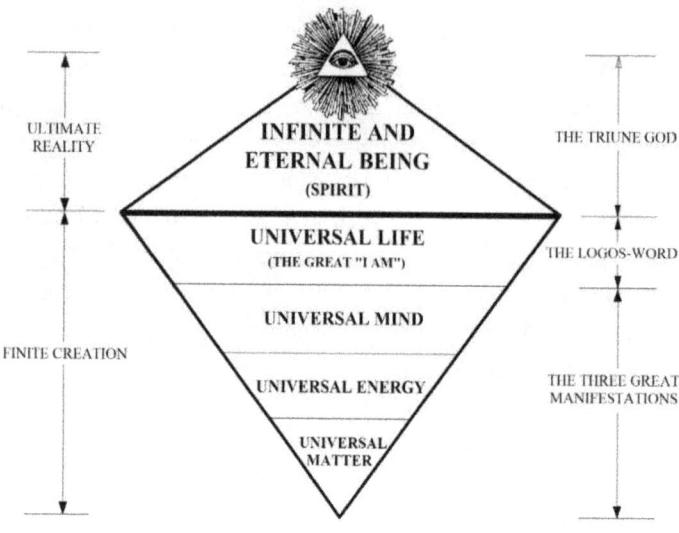

Figure 3: The Various Vibratory Levels in Existence

7.7 The One God as a Unified Trinity of Divine Persons

Spirit vibration is infinitely beyond anything that can be experienced in the entire universe. In fact, as compared to anything in creation, spirit vibration is so rapid as to appear perfectly still and at complete rest. Nevertheless, no matter how rapid, where there is vibration there is also rhythm; and this also applies to divine spirit. In reality, the reason why vibration and rhythm pervade the entire universe is because the universe faithfully reflects the vibratory and rhythmic nature of divine spirit.

Similar to vibration, compared to what is experienced as real in the universe, divine spirit is "hyper-real." Moreover, divine spirit is not simply living, it is "totally alive" to an infinite degree. Divine spirit is life itself. Furthermore, as difficult as it is for us to imagine, divine spirit is infinitely more than simply self-existent, it is total being—pure aseity. Consequently, at the transcendent level of divine spirit, the three requirements of vibration and rhythm are not simply mechanical forces (as in the physical world), or universal principles (as in the mental world), but actual beings—divine persons.

At the numinous level of divine spirit, contractive action towards an inner centre is the function of the divine person known esoterically as the "Heavenly Father." The expansive action towards an outer periphery is the function of the divine person known esoterically as the "Holy Mother." The mutual interaction of the Heavenly Father and the Holy Mother generates a perfect union that is esoterically known as the "Eternal Son."[31] Of course, it is understood here that human terms relating to gender and family are raised to infinite perfection when applied to God.

The Heavenly Father's inward point of concentration is the identity of God, or "divine being." The Holy Mother's outward inclusion of all is the wisdom of God, or "divine knowing." The rhythmic, interactive union of divine being and divine knowing generates the self-consciousness of God, or the "divine self-awareness" of the Eternal Son (for a diagrammatic representation of the divine Trinity, please refer to Figure 4 on the following page).

The rhythmic, perfectly balanced interaction of the three divine persons should not be regarded as a mere mechanical-style vibration; but more correctly as a loving familial relationship that has been mutually enjoyed throughout eternity. In truth, the term "divine love" is synonymous with the spirit of God. Moreover, the harmonious alternation from divine being to divine knowing occurs with such infinite rapidity, that each divine person is in perfect union with the others.[32]

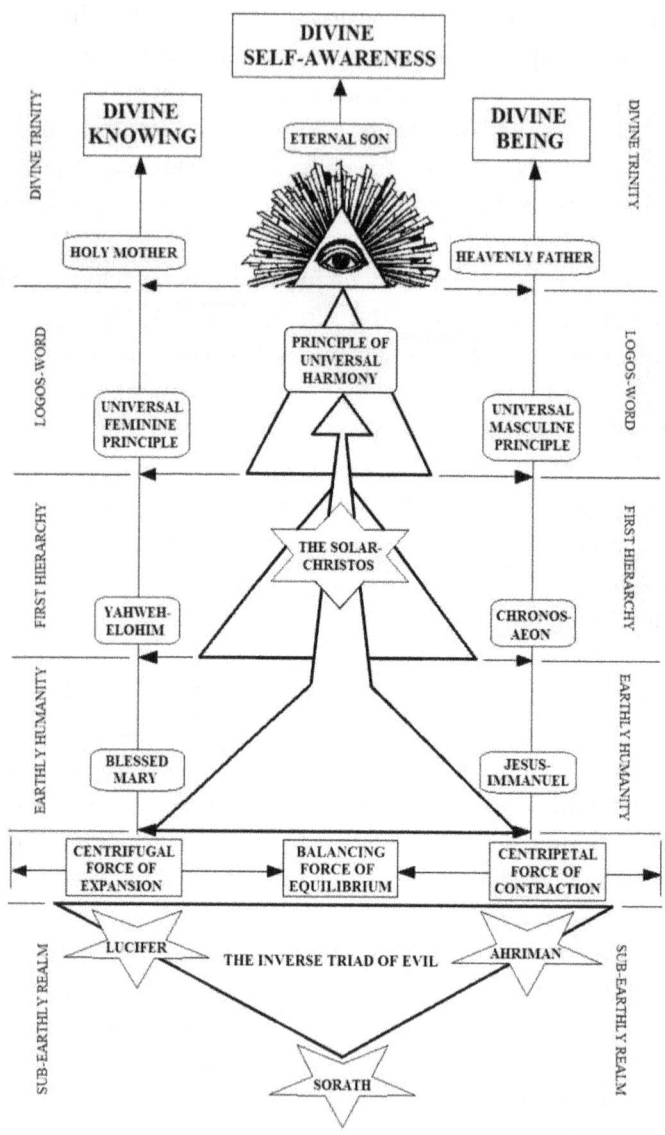

Figure 4: The Universal Principle of Triplicity

7.8 The Inverse Triad of Evil

Now that we have esoterically considered the trinitarian nature of the divine Creator and how it is reflected within various vibratory levels of the universe, we are better prepared to understand how and why the universal principle of triplicity also applies to those beings who have chosen to forge a dark path of evil. From the identifiable characteristics of Lucifer, Ahriman and Sorath (that were previously discussed in Chapters 4, 5 and 6), it should be apparent at this point that together they form an inverted, sub-earthly distortion of the divine Trinity (please refer to Figure 4 on the previous page).

By taking the centrifugal force of expansion to an outward extreme, Lucifer exaggerates and distorts the universal feminine principle, which is a reflection of the Holy Mother. Lucifer, then, is the evil opponent of the Holy Mother. Moreover, since the Holy Mother is the deific personification of divine knowing, or the "wisdom of God," Lucifer exaggerates and distorts universal wisdom. This of course is consistent with the esoteric knowledge that Lucifer is a regressed spirit of wisdom.

In Ahriman's case, by taking the centripetal force of contraction to an inward extreme, he exaggerates and distorts the universal masculine principle, which is a reflection of the Heavenly Father. Ahriman, then, is the evil opponent of the Heavenly Father. Moreover, since the Heavenly Father is the deific personification of divine being, or the "will of God," Ahriman exaggerates and distorts universal will. This is also consistent with the esoteric knowledge that Ahriman is a regressed "power," or spirit of form.

Sorath, as we know, is the self-declared opponent of the Solar-Christos, and is consequently known as the "Sun-Demon." Since the Solar-Christos embodies and manifests the principle of universal harmony to a supernal degree, and since this principle is a reflection of the Eternal Son, Sorath has become the evil opponent of the Eternal Son. Rather than promoting universal harmony and the balancing force of equilibrium, Sorath promotes universal disharmony and imbalance. Instead of harmoniously reigning-in the polarizing excesses of Lucifer and Ahriman, Sorath continues to encourage and promote their extremist activities. By positioning himself at the centre of the earth, Sorath occupies a central position of power over the radical polarities of Lucifer and Ahriman.

It's unfortunate for suffering humanity that Lucifer, Ahriman and Sorath don't willingly curtail their extremist activities. If they would maintained their own applications of universal vibratory force within appropriate boundaries, they would be beneficial to human and earthly development. Lucifer, for example, could be an agent of the Holy Spirit instead of her enemy.[33] Ahriman could promote the will of the Father instead of opposing it. Sorath could be a "sun-friend," instead of a "sun-fiend."

CHAPTER 8

CELESTIAL BENEFACTORS OF MANKIND: THE SOLAR-CHRISTOS

8.1 The Foremost Benefactor of Mankind: The Solar-Christos

EVEN THOUGH the three proximate perpetrators of evil towards mankind—Lucifer, Ahriman and Sorath—are regressive in their own developments, they are all still much more powerful than ordinary human beings. Throughout history, humanity would have been quite defenseless against their evil onslaught if it weren't for the benevolent, overarching protection and guidance of other highly-advanced beings. Foremost among these great celestial benefactors is the exalted spirit of the sun, the Solar-Christos (also known simply as, "the Christ").

Even though as the leader of the sun-spirits, the Solar-Christos oversees the progressive development of our entire solar system, throughout history he has taken a particular loving concern for the plight of fledgling humanity. As previously discussed in Chapter 4, the Solar-Christos has on several occasions directly intervened in human evolution in order to counteract the evil machinations of Lucifer, Ahriman and Sorath. Once in ancient Lemurian times, twice during the great Atlantean Age, and once during the Graeco-Roman cultural era, the Solar-Christos indwelt a specially-prepared human being (later to be known as "Jesus-Immanuel") in order to *internally* assist humanity on earth, and not just *externally* from his home on the sun.

The indwelling of the Solar-Logos in the person of Christ-Jesus, just a little over two thousand years ago, marked a momentous turning point in human history. Up to that point, humanity was descending deeper and deeper into earthly materiality, with the risk of forever losing its connection to the spiritual world. Through his indwelling presence in the body and soul of Jesus-Immanuel, the Solar-Christos was able to access and apply the superplanetary forces of the sun, the macrocosmic forces of the Logos-Word, and the divine forces of the Son-God for the redemption and salvation of desperate mankind.

Because of his world-altering incarnation as Christ-Jesus, the Solar-Christos was able to rescue the archetype of the human body (the "physical phantom") from the mineralizing grip of Sorath; which thereby ensures the positive future development of the human ego on earth. Furthermore, by undergoing the horrific experience of death on the cross, the Solar-Christos was able to superphysically descend to the very centre of the earth; and thereby blaze a pathway of divine light and love into the debased heart of Sorath's black domain.[34]

By bringing the mystic star of his God-Self to the centre of the earth, the Solar-Logos ignited the earth's potential to become a planetary-sun, and to one day re-unite with the great central sun of our system. The seed-spark of a future sun that was planted at the centre of the earth also began the process of transmuting Sorath's corrupt and degenerate matter and energy. Over time, this transmutation will increasingly remove Sorath's power of black-magic, and will increasingly surround and contain him in a sub-earthly enclosure of divine protective light. Sadly, however, the bright light of truth is painfully revealing to evil souls who revel in spiritual darkness; such that they do whatever they can to run and hide from the light, to "blind" themselves to the light of truth.

Unlike the typical process of spirit-indwelling, where the more advanced being only permeates the soul of the host-individual for a short period of time, the Solar-Christos has selflessly chosen to remain inwardly united with Jesus-Immanuel until the "end of the age." By doing so, the Solar-Christos has assumed the additional responsibility of becoming the new planetary-spirit of the earth. In this capacity, he is labouring to transform the entire planet into the "new earth"; and by doing so, transform the entire solar system into the "new heaven."

In a very real sense, then, the resurrection of Christ-Jesus heralded the "end of the world"; that is, the end of the old world-order, and the beginning of the new. For this reason, spiritual science refers to this momentous event as "the turning-point of time." The Catholic Church has also recognized the world-altering significance of the resurrection by referring to it as the dawning of the "eighth day of creation." As stated in paragraph 349 of the *Catechism of the Catholic Church* (2000):

> The eighth day. But for us a new day has dawned: the day of Christ's Resurrection. The seventh day completes the first creation. The eighth day begins the new creation. Thus, the work of creation culminates in the greater work of redemption. The first creation finds its meaning and its summit in the new creation in Christ, the splendour of which surpasses that of the first creation.

8.2 The Solar-Christos and Lucifer are *Not* Celestial Brothers

A subtly-pernicious misconception that continues to be naively promulgated by numerous present-day esotericists, including anthroposophists, is that the Solar-Christos (Christ) and Lucifer are amicable celestial "brothers." In one sense it is true that since we are all children of God, this makes us all spiritual brothers and sisters. But this is not what is being esoterically implied with Christ and Lucifer. The erroneous implication is that these two advanced beings are on an equal developmental footing, and that both are equally beneficial to human evolution. Nothing could be further from the truth.

In regard to the Solar-Christos, even though he is an archangelic being, over long ages of faithful obedience to the divine will, and by the dedicated expression of selfless divine love towards others, he has advanced to the level of a virtue or spirit of movement (please refer to Figure 5 on the following page). Lucifer, on the other hand, properly belongs with the dominions or spirits of wisdom; but because he has for long ages opposed the divine will, and selfishly cared more for himself than for others, he has regressed and fallen back to the level of a virtue. So, even though both advanced beings are virtues, the Solar-Christos is on an ascending line of evolution, while Lucifer is on a descending line of devolution. This hardly makes them "equal brothers."

Even as far back in time as the Ancient Sun Period of earth development, when Lucifer was still the planetary-spirit of Venus and the Solar-Christos was the burgeoning planetary-spirit of the sun, they were hardly amicable brothers. In fact, there was fierce opposition between the two beings, and even though the Solar-Christos was victorious in the struggle, it took all his spiritual effort of will to do so. In consequence, Lucifer was removed as the planetary-spirit of Venus and exiled to the earth.

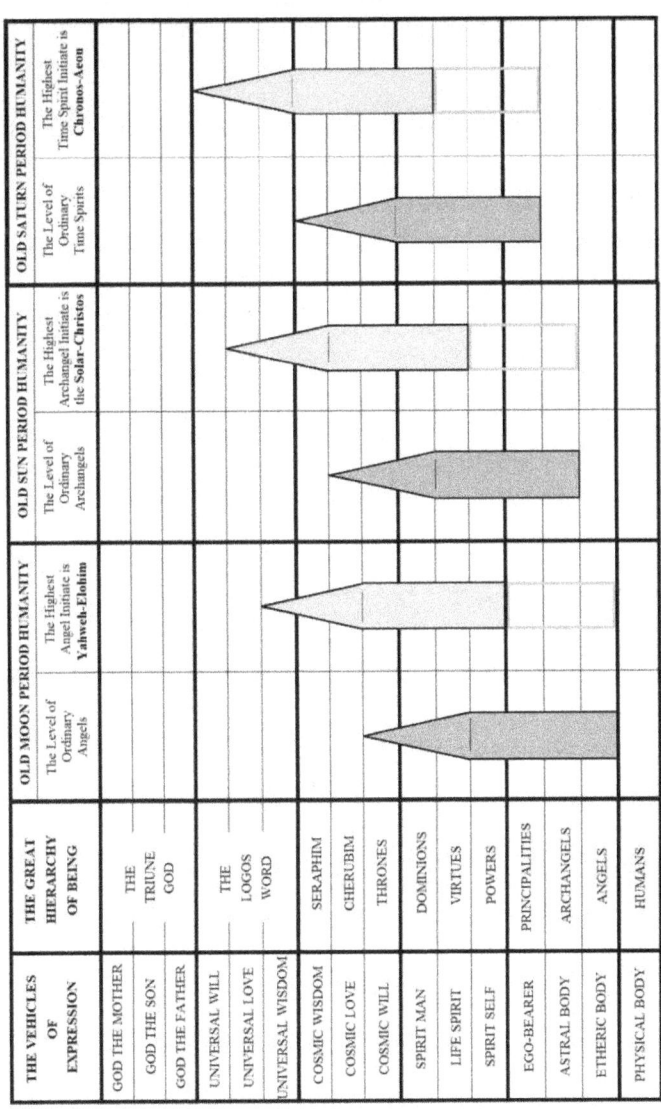

Figure 5: Hierarchic Levels of Development

Speaking of these events in a lecture given on 12 June 1912, and published in *Man in the Light of Occultism, Theosophy and Philosophy* (1989), Rudolf Steiner presented the following noteworthy details:

> We learn how Christ already on the old Moon overcame Lucifer ... Christ attained to victory over Lucifer. On Earth Christ repels Lucifer from the outset. This is because on the Moon, when He was Himself less highly evolved—for Christ also undergoes evolution—He had repelled, through the uttermost devotion of His Being to the Highest Powers, all the attacks of Lucifer which at that time still meant something to Him. Already on old Moon Lucifer approached Christ. On Earth he was no longer dangerous to Him: on Earth Christ repels Lucifer at once. On the Moon, however, Christ had to exert all the forces at His disposal in order to repel Lucifer.
>
> When we go back to the time of the old Sun ... We find the Sun still as a planet among the seven planets, we find Venus with Lucifer as her ruler; and these two, the Sun Spirit and the Venus Spirit—in other words, Christ and Lucifer—appear at first sight like brothers. Only by straining to the utmost our powers of perception are we able to remark the difference between them.
>
> Lucifer is a Spirit endowed in his very nature with infinite pride, so great a pride that it can prove a temptation to man ...
>
> And how does the Christ figure look beside Lucifer? The Christ figure in the time of old Sun—the Lord and Ruler of the Sun planet—is a picture of utmost devotion, entire devotion to all that is around Him in the world. Whereas Lucifer looks like one who thinks only of himself ... Christ appears as wholly given up, in devotion, to all that is around Him in the great wide world.

Christ on the other hand gave Himself up to the impression of this Word of the worlds, received It in its fullness and entirety into Himself, so that this Christ Soul was now the Being that united in Himself all the great secrets of the world that sounded into Him through the inexpressible Word.

Such is the contrast that presents itself: the Christ Who receives the Word of the worlds, and the proud Lucifer, the Spirit of Venus, who rejects the Word of the worlds and wants to found and establish everything with his own light.

All subsequent evolution is a direct outcome of what Lucifer and Christ were at that time.

From the preceding quotation, Rudolf Steiner makes it abundantly clear that the Solar-Christos and Lucifer are *not* amicable spirit-brothers: externally, they only *appear* to be brothers; internally they are diametrically-opposed adversaries, and will continue to be so far into the future.

8.3 The Solar-Christos is Already Victorious Over the Evil Triad of Lucifer, Ahriman and Sorath

As indicated by the spiritual-scientific research of Rudolf Steiner, the Solar-Christos has been entirely victorious over Lucifer since the Ancient Moon Period. In Ahriman's case, victory has only been achieved during the present Earth Period; because in previous periods, Ahriman was not an evil factor in human development. Regarding Sorath, the Solar-Christos was only able to overcome him by superphysically confronting him at the earth's core, following his sacrificial death on the cross.

As amazing as it sounds to the materialistic-minded, the Solar-Christos has been able to overcome the powerful combined forces of the triad of evil entirely on the strength of the light of divine truth and the warmth of divine love. The Solar-Christos bears no malice towards his adversaries; he has only an all-embracing compassion towards them. But it's this blazing purity of numinous truth and love that causes these highly-advanced but evilly-inclined beings to hurl themselves into the deep abyss in an effort to conceal and enclose themselves within a "protective enclosure" of darkness. Unfortunately, it's this very enclosure that keeps them enchained and imprisoned.

In a lecture given on 18 May 1915, when discussing his large wooden sculpture that depicts Christ in relation to Lucifer and Ahriman (presently displayed in the Goetheanum at Dornach, Switzerland), Rudolf Steiner similarly remarked:

> [A]nother figure, winged but with his wings broken, who for this reason begins to fall into the abyss ... It must not appear, however, as if the Christ Himself were breaking the wings of this being. Rather, ... the Christ, by the very motion of raising his hand, is expressing his infinite compassion for this being ... When this being comes into proximity with the Christ being, he feels something that may be expressed in the words: "I cannot bear the radiation of such purity upon me."
>
> This feeling dominates so essentially as to break this upper being's wings and cause his imminent plunge into the abyss ... Rather, the being must be portrayed as having caused his own fall, for what is to be shown plunging downward, with broken wings, is Lucifer.
>
> Again, it will be ... important ... not to show the Christ as wanting to shackle this figure; rather, he has infinite compassion for this being, which is Ahriman. Ahriman cannot bear this compassion and he writhes with pain from what the hand of the Christ exudes. This radiance from Christ's hand causes the golden veins down in the

rock depression to wind around Ahriman's body like strong cords and shackle him. (From the lecture published in *Christ in Relation to Lucifer and Ahriman*; 1978)

Even though the divine power radiating from the Solar-Christos has caused Lucifer, Ahriman and Sorath to imprison themselves in the foul darkness of the subterranean abyss, this does not mean that these beings can no longer influence and corrupt unsuspecting humanity. Individual human beings (and thereby, humanity as a whole) can only effectively protect themselves from the still-powerful triad of evil by uniting themselves with the Solar-Christos. Otherwise, the force of evil issuing from these highly-advanced but malevolent spirit-beings will prove far too strong and invincible for undeveloped human beings.

Furthermore, as the Solar-Christos continues to irradiate the earth's interior and transform the planet into a microcosmic source of light (a "planetary-sun"), then it will become increasingly more difficult for the evil triad to imprison themselves in sub-earthly darkness. Eventually they will have to flee to another source of sub-material darkness, or discontinue their evil ways. Hopefully soon, the three principal perpetrators of evil—Lucifer, Ahriman and Sorath—will choose to be redeemed, and begin to follow a path of holiness instead of a path of evil.

Part of our difficulty as human beings is that advanced beings have a very different relationship to time than we do. As biblically expressed in 2 Peter 3:8: "But do not ignore this one fact, beloved, that with the Lord one day is as a thousand years, and a thousand years as one day." Similarly with supernatural beings such as Lucifer, Ahriman and Sorath. Even though it may take a short period of superphysical-time for them to repent, it could mean thousands of years of human-time for this welcomed repentance to be noticed on earth.

8.4 The Solar-Christos as the Harmonizing Protection from the Extremes of Evil

The harsh reality of today's world is that Lucifer, Ahriman and Sorath have insinuated themselves into the very fabric of earthly life—into our bodies, into our souls, into our society, into our culture, into our natural environment, and into our technology. It is obvious, therefore, that human beings cannot avoid evil by running away from Lucifer, Ahriman and Sorath, since they are present everywhere we go.[35] So how then are we to effectively deal with supernatural evil?

The only viable option is to face them "head-on"; that is, to confront them directly when we consciously encounter them, resist their evil machinations; and by doing so, overcome them. However, to do this on our own would be futile and ineffective; to successfully overcome supernatural evil, human beings need to be protectively armed with the superior power of the Solar-Christos.

Even though his lower ego-bearing vehicle remains tethered to the earth through Jesus-Immanuel, the highest vehicle of the Solar-Christos extends to the macrocosmic level of the Logos-Word (please refer to Figures 4 and 5). In consequence, the Solar-Christos germinally embodies the harmonizing principle of universal love, which enables him to spiritually balance the feminine principle of universal expansion and the masculine principle of universal contraction. The Solar-Christos, then, has the macrocosmic power to prevent Lucifer from outwardly expanding to a distorted and damaging degree; and to prevent Ahriman from inwardly contracting to a distorted and damaging degree. Moreover, the Solar-Christos also has the power to neutralize the chaotic, disharmonizing activity of Sorath.

As long as the Solar-Christos properly contains and restricts the extremist tendencies of Lucifer, Ahriman and Sorath, their actions are not destructive or injurious to mankind.³⁶ This does not mean that these powerfully-malevolent beings suddenly become friendly benefactors to mankind. Preventing them from doing human injury does not change that fact that they still intend to do serious harm to humanity if left unchecked. Moreover, negating Sorath's power of discord with the harmonizing power of the Solar-Christos, and then forcefully arresting the extremist tendencies of Lucifer and Ahriman, also does not mean that the triad of evil has been miraculously redeemed. To be truly redeemed, each spirit-being of the evil triad needs to repent with a sincere contriteness of heart. As well, they need to take responsibility for their evil actions, and seek to make recompense for the karmic damage they have done over vast stretches of time. Lastly, they must solemnly vow to God that they will sincerely end their evil ways. Unfortunately for Lucifer, Ahriman and Sorath, on the cosmic game-board of life, there is no "get out of hell for free" card.³⁷

To state once again, the Solar-Christos has the power to supersede Sorath and to reign-in the extremist polarizations of Lucifer and Ahriman. But it must also be clearly understood at this point, that the Solar-Christos has benevolently overcome the evil powers of Lucifer, Ahriman and Sorath in his *own* life. He has *not* done this on a planetary scale for the whole of humanity. To do so would have negated each person's capacity of free-will. The Solar-Christos has provided every human being with the ability and opportunity to overcome and vanquish evil on their own. But to do this, each person must freely choose to enlist his benevolent spiritual assistance.

With the power of the Solar-Christos indwelling their own soul, the faithful Christian can freely walk a straight and narrow path of holiness through life on earth, without being Sorathically expanded to a Luciferic extreme, or Sorathically contracted to an Ahrimanic extreme. With the inner power of the Solar-Christos, the faithful Christian is able to confront the powerfully-evil beings of the inverse triad "face-to-face," and successfully overcome their extremist temptations. Together with Christ-Jesus, the dedicated disciple can confidently declare: "Get thee behind me, Satan ... Lucifer and Sorath."

8.5 Mankind Does Not Need Lucifer, Ahriman and Sorath in Order to Exist in the World

Just because complacent mankind has become materially dependent on the numerous evil manifestations to be found in modern-life—such as electricity, magnetism and nuclear power—does not mean that human beings need Lucifer, Ahriman and Sorath in order to exist in this world. It's important to remember that the universe is a divine creation; and as such, is entirely dependent on the will, wisdom and love of God for its existence. Moreover, we as human beings are dependent on a great many things for our existence on earth; such as air, water, food, clothing, shelter, companionship and sunlight. But all our necessities ultimately derive from God.

Therefore, whatever has been created by Lucifer, Ahriman or Sorath does not belong exclusively to them; it belongs to the entire universe (the Logos-Word), and ultimately to God. Moreover, considering the vibratory nature of the whole universe, mankind is certainly dependent on the universal feminine forces of expansion, together with the universal masculine forces of contraction. But these forces don't exclusively belong to Lucifer, or to Ahriman. Furthermore, while it's also necessary to maintain a healthy and positive balance between these essential forces; that ability (or rather, the distortion of that ability) certainly doesn't belong entirely to Sorath.

When it becomes necessary to engage one or the other

forces of expansion, contraction or equilibrium, human beings are not compelled to singularly enlist the "services" of Lucifer, Ahriman or Sorath. There are a great many benevolent beings who also embody theses forces, who don't take them to extremes, and who are eminently more trustworthy than the triad of evil. For instance, Blessed Mary, the archangel Gabriel[38] and Yahweh-Elohim (the spirit of the moon) each primarily embody the expansive feminine forces of the Holy Mother. Jesus-Immanuel, Michael the Archai and Chronos-Aeon (the spirit of Saturn, aka "Father Time") each primarily embody the contractive masculine forces of the Heavenly Father. And of course, the Solar-Christos best embodies the compassionate harmonizing forces of the Eternal Son. Rather than pitting the forces of Lucifer and Ahriman against each other in order to achieve a healthy balance in life, esotericists need to re-think this strategy and begin employing a more positive approach.

8.6 An Alternative to the "Polar-Opposite Method" of Counterbalancing Lucifer and Ahriman

Since ancient times, esotericists have known and applied the "Hermetic principle of polarity" in order to cultivate and maintain a healthy balance in their lives.[39] As a general description to illustrate this principle, when the experienced esotericist is confronted with a particular undesirable or harmful force, that force can be negated or neutralized by centrally positioning oneself between its polar opposite. In other words, by counteracting one particular force with its polar opposite, a balanced equilibrium can be achieved. A simple example is a room that is excessively cold. By introducing excessive heat for an appropriate period of time, a balanced temperature can be obtained.

No doubt with this principle of polarity in mind, the

eminent esotericist, Rudolf Steiner, in many of his lectures, promoted a similar strategy for contemporary human beings to deal with Lucifer and Ahriman. Statements made in a lecture given in 18 May 1915, and later published in *Christ in Relation to Lucifer and Ahriman* (1978), provide one such example:

> Rather, everything that man has to strive for as a result of the Christ impulse must be seen as similar to the equilibrious state of a pendulum. In the center, the pendulum is in perfect balance, but it must oscillate to one side or the other. The same applies to man's development here on earth. Man must oscillate to the one side according to the luciferic principle and to the other according to the principle of Ahriman, but he must maintain his equilibrium through the cultivation of Paul's declaration, "Not I, but Christ in me."

Another representative example was provided in a lecture given on 25 August 1913, which stated the following:

> These beings we call Ahriman and Lucifer are right here in the world, they have their task in the universal order, and one cannot sweep them away. Besides, it is not a question of annihilating them, but—as in the case of the weights on both sides of the scales—the ahrimanic and luciferic forces must balance each other in their influence on human beings and on other beings. (Published in *Secrets of the Threshold*; 1987)

There is no question, that in a world such as ours where Lucifer, Ahriman and Sorath are active all around us—and even in us—that a certain balance can be achieved by counteracting Luciferic forces with opposing Ahrimanic forces, and thereby neutralizing Sorath's evil forces at the centre. The problem with this otherwise-effective strategy is that we are always calling to mind one or another evil-spirit to obtain a proper balance in the world. In a sense, then, the perpetrators of evil are strengthened by the fact that we are constantly focused on them.

This approach is somewhat analogous to maintaining a healthy garden by exclusively focusing on removing the weeds. While focusing on the weeds will certainly be effective, the downside is that the enjoyment of the healthy plants is almost forgotten by the constant attention to the weeds. An equally effective method of cultivating a healthy garden is to focus attention on the healthy plants, and work to promote them. Over time, the increased growth of the healthy plants will naturally crowd out the weeds. And most importantly with this alternative approach, concentration is focused on the positive, rather than the negative.

Illustrating this alternative approach with the previous example of an excessively cold room. One doesn't need to counteractively apply excessive heat in order to have a balanced temperature. One can also apply a gentler heat for a longer period of time, which will also result in an evenly-balanced, room temperature.

8.7 Avoiding the Evil Excesses in Life by Focusing on the Divine Trinity

To illustrate how this alternative approach would apply to Lucifer and Ahriman, an example will be taken from a lecture given by Rudolf Steiner on 22 November 1914, and published in *The Balance in the World and Man: Lucifer and Ahriman* (1977). The example taken is about "duty." It is stated here, that if a person merely "fulfills his duty" in a cold, hard and uninspired way, then he is a slave to duty; and "He hardens in an Ahrimanic sense, notwithstanding that he follows duty devotedly."

In this example, the cold Ahrimanic attitude towards duty

is brought into balance by counteracting it with the warming self-love of Lucifer. As stated in the lecture:

> [I]f we bring all our power of self-love—as an offering and offer it up to duty, bringing thus to duty the Luciferic warmth of love, then the result is that, through the state of balance induced in this way between Lucifer and Ahriman, we find a right relation to duty

In accordance with the principle of polarity, this particular strategy will certainly work to bring about a healthier balance. Nevertheless, an alternative approach can be equally successful on the basis that the universal forces of feminine expansion and masculine contraction aren't the exclusive property of Lucifer and Ahriman; but are reflections of the divine Trinity. Therefore, a cold and Ahrimanic hardness of attitude towards one's duty can also be effectively balanced by spiritually engaging the warming love of the Holy Mother.

With this alternative approach, it isn't necessary to balance the excesses of one evil-being with the excesses of an opposing evil-being. The extremes of Lucifer can be counterbalanced by the Heavenly Father; the extremes of Ahriman can be counterbalanced by the Holy Mother; and the extremes of Sorath can be counterbalance by the Eternal Son.

Considering that the inverse triad of evil (that is, Lucifer, Ahriman and Sorath) is a corrupted and debased reflection of the divine Trinity (that is, the Holy Mother, the Heavenly Father and the Eternal Son), it makes perfect sense to counteract the evil excesses of the inverse triad with the benevolent power of the divine Trinity.

8.8 Achieving Spiritual Balance and Equipoise by Centering on Christ-Jesus

Along the same line as the "Trinitarian approach" to counterbalance evil—but from a slightly different perspective—is to spiritually unite with Christ-Jesus. By doing so, the superplanetary power of the Solar-Christos begins to radiate from the very centre of one's being. Since the superconsciousness of the Solar-Christos reaches as high as the Logos-Word, and since the Logos-Word is supernally infused with the harmonizing love of the Eternal Son, uniting with Christ-Jesus is like riding a high-speed elevator to the top of creation, a veritable fast-track to God.

With the combined harmonizing power of Christ-Jesus, the Solar-Christos, the Logos-Word and the Eternal Son at the very centre of one's life and being, such a "winning" combination is supernally sufficient to provide the necessary calm and equipoise in any raging conflagration of evil. Besides, since Christ-Jesus has been divinely granted victorious authority over the triad of evil, his presence in the very heart of our soul is ample power to push back and fence off the evil intrusions of Lucifer, Ahriman and Sorath.

8.9 The Harmonizing Radiance of Christ-Jesus from the Sacred Cube of the Heart

In a lecture given on 21 November 1914, and published in *The Balance in the World and Man: Lucifer and Ahriman* (1977), Rudolf Steiner described in detail how Lucifer and Ahriman attempt to make evil intrusion into the physical human body. These evil assaults are made from the six main directions of three-dimensional space: Lucifer from the left, and Ahriman from the right; Lucifer from the front, and Ahriman from the back; and Lucifer from above, and Ahriman from below (please refer to Figure 6 on the following page).

As a protective barrier against these forced invasions, the progressive spirits—particularly Yahweh-Elohim—established a sacred, three-dimensional cube within the bodily torso where evil forces couldn't intrude. As stated in the lecture:

> [T]here, in the middle, where Jehovah created man, as it were in the form of a cube. There it was that he so filled man with His own being, with His own magic breath, that the influence of this magic breath was able to extend into the regions in the rest of man that belong to Lucifer and Ahriman. Here in the midst, bounded above and below and before and behind, is an intervening space where the breath of Jehovah enters directly into the spatial human being.

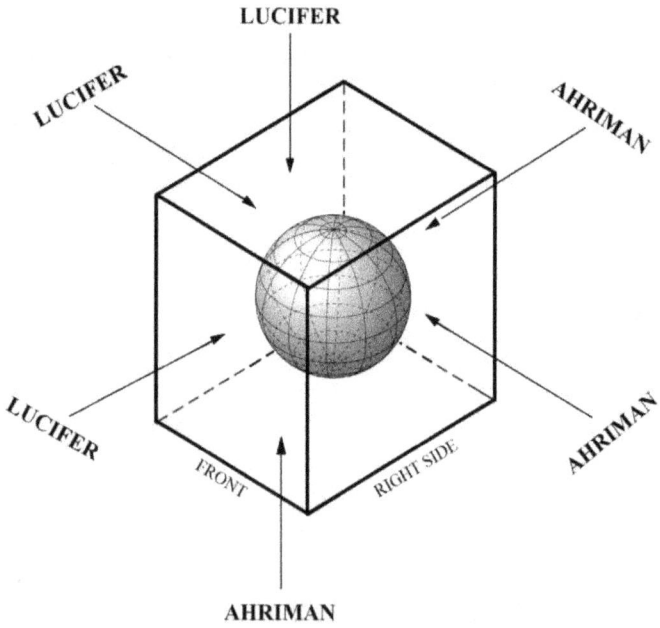

Figure 6: Evil Attacks on the Physical Body in Three-Dimensional Space

Once we have spiritually united ourselves with Christ-Jesus, this sacred cube surrounding our heart becomes enflamed with the power of the Son—with the power of divine love.[40] This divine radiance is repellent to evil, which hastily flees in all directions of three-dimensional space. Once again, rather than attempting to balance one evil with another, Christ-Jesus offers the safest and most effective spiritual protection against the inverse triad of evil. The spiritual wisdom of this approach has been intuitively expressed in the words of a traditional Christian hymn entitled "Christ Be Beside Me":

Christ be beside me, Christ be before me,
Christ be behind me, King of my heart;
Christ be within me, Christ be below me,
Christ be above me, never to part.

Christ on my right hand, Christ on my left hand,
Christ all around me, shield in the strife;
Christ in my sleeping, Christ in my sitting,
Christ in my rising, light of my heart.

CHAPTER 9

CELESTIAL BENEFACTORS OF MANKIND: YAHWEH-ELOHIM

9.1 Yahweh-Elohim: The Advanced Leader of the Angelic Kingdom

OF ALL THE GREAT celestial benefactors of mankind, few have endured more disrespectful treatment by esotericists than Yahweh-Elohim. The ancient Gnostics falsely accused him of being the "Demiurge" (or "Ialdabaoth"), a flawed, malevolent deity who supposedly created a depraved and corrupted material world. In the writings of the Theosophical Society, a similar diatribe against Yahweh was often expressed. In *The Secret Doctrine: Volume II—Anthropogenesis* (2011), H.P. Blavatsky (1831–1891) wrote the following:

> The Beings, or the Being, collectively called Elohim [that is, Yahweh-Elohim]... must have been indeed that Ildabaoth, the Demiurge of the Nazarenes, filled with rage and envy against his own creature ... In this case it is but natural ... to view Satan, the Serpent of Genesis, as the real creator and benefactor, the Father of Spiritual

mankind. For it is he who was the 'Harbinger of Light', bright radiant Lucifer, who opened the eyes of the automaton created by Jehovah ... can only be personated in the light of a Saviour. An 'adversary' to Jehovah the 'personating spirit.'

It is clear from these two sources, that those esotericists who castigate Yahweh-Elohim, usually mistakenly believe that Lucifer/Satan is the great benefactor of mankind, and that Yahweh is somehow the villain. For this reason, it's necessary at this point to set the record straight about who is the truly trustworthy friend to humanity, and who is the spurious imposter.

According to Rosicrucian wisdom, Yahweh-Elohim is a highly-advanced angel-being who has progressed to the hierarchic level of a power or spirit of form (please refer to Figure 5). As such, he is the current leader of the progressive angels who promote the divinely-ordained world order. In this capacity, Yahweh-Elohim has greatly assisted struggling mankind, and has repeatedly provided protection from the onslaughts of the triad of evil.

No doubt, one of the main reasons that the exalted leader of the angels has been historically vilified by Lucifer and his Gnostic and Theosophical supporters, is because Yahweh-Elohim has been crucially instrumental in thwarting Lucifer's attempts to establish a counterfeit planet within the solar system.

9.2 Yahweh-Elohim and the Formation of the Moon

At a certain point in the Lemurian Age, powerfully-atavistic etheric debris left over from the Ancient Moon period was increasingly causing a life-threatening densification and rigidification of the entire earth. To maintain planetary life and to continue positive human development, these mummifying forces needed to be ejected to a safe spherical distance away from the earth. At the orbital boundary of this sphere of Old Moon residue, Lucifer saw an opportunity to congeal a renegade planet, as a secondary substitute to replace his exiled home on Venus.

Unfortunately for Lucifer and company, Yahweh-Elohim and his celestial companions from the sun completely thwarted the formation of Lucifer's illegitimate "eighth sphere" by materializing the present lunar orb instead. As the planetary-spirit of the moon, Yahweh-Elohim has steadfastly laboured to prevent Lucifer from using the same space for his own runaway planet. Consequently, Lucifer's renegade eighth sphere only exists as a ghostly, unmaterialized realm of hallucinatory images and phantom forms that invisibly surrounds the earth.

9.3 Yahweh-Elohim and the Anti-Luciferic Functions of Heredity and Tribal Love

Some misinformed esotericists have disparagingly described Yahweh-Elohim as a "tribal deity." While there is certainly some truth to the description, it is in a positive sense and not a negative one. Once again, in ancient Lemurian times, in order to counteract Lucifer's seductive astral-infusion of egotistical self-love and independence, Yahweh-Elohim introduced the reproductive forces of heredity and the social strictures of tribal love.

Lucifer's nefarious intention for encouraging selfish independence and selfish love was not to develop true personal freedom for humanity; but instead, to loosen human beings from their evolutionary attraction to the earth, in order to covertly transfer them to his intended bogus planet. To prevent this from happening, Yahweh-Elohim and the progressive moon-beings generationally anchored physical bodies to the earth through the reproductive forces of heredity. As well, human attention was diverted from selfish love to tribal love; that is, individual selfhood was identified with families, tribes and communities instead of one's separate ego. As explained by Rudolf Steiner in a lecture given on 26 October 1917 entitled "The Spirits of Light and the Spirits of Darkness":

> Anything to do with physical heredity was given to humanity by the spirits of light to counterbalance the luciferic stream. A weight was attached to human beings, as it were, and this connected them with the earth. In everything connected with heredity, with the begetting of children, procreation, with love in the earthly sense, we must therefore see ourselves connected with the entities which are under the leadership of Yahveh or Jehovah.
>
> The laws of Judaism—which was to prepare the way for Christianity—as well as those of pagan religions, clearly show the importance attached to regulating everything to do with the laws of heredity here on earth. People had to learn to live together in tribes, nations and races, with blood relationship as the signature for the way affairs were ordered on earth. (Published in *The Fall of the Spirits of Darkness*, 1996)

Eventually, once mankind was more advanced and resistant to Luciferic assault, the divine forces incarnate in Christ-Jesus would supersede the socially-tethering forces of tribalism and genetics, and begin to develop the socially-liberating forces of universal love and true, personal selfhood.

9.4 Under the Direction of Christ-Jesus, Yahweh-Elohim Now Promotes True Personal Freedom

As indicated in the previous quotation by H.P. Blavatsky,

esoteric critics of Yahweh-Elohim, in spite of their animosity, do acknowledge that the elohim "created" human beings. However, they mistakenly believe that Yahweh (Jehovah) and the other elohim merely created an "automaton"; that is, a soulless creature entirely devoid of selfhood and free-independence. And of course, they also mistakenly believe that it was "bright radiant Lucifer" who "opened the eyes" of mankind; that is, who instilled self-conscious awareness and free-will in human beings.

According to the clairvoyant research of spiritual science, the preceding view of human creation is a specious, Luciferic distortion of the actual events. During the Ancient Moon period of earth development, the spirits of form (elohim) were certainly instrumental in "formulating" our human ancestors. At that particular evolutionary stage, our human precursors were indeed "animal-like"; that is, separate human forms did not possess an individualized ego-bearing soul; but instead, were instinctually directed by a group-soul.

So, while it is correctly understood that primordial humanity did not possess individualized selfhood and personal free-will, this is best understood as a temporary, animal-like stage of human evolution, rather than as a permanent, automaton condition of humanoid existence. It was never intended by the elohim (or the other progressive celestial beings) that humanity permanently remain at an animal-like stage of evolution. Rather, it is the divine will of creation to raise up truly free and fully self-conscious beings, not soulless automatons.

In accordance with this divine directive, during the Lemurian Age of our Present Earth period of evolution, Yahweh and his fellow elohim sacrificially "gifted" our animal-like human ancestors with an individualized ego-bearing soul. To be perfectly clear, then, it was not Lucifer and his rebel spirits who granted an immortal soul to nascent humanity; it was Yahweh-Elohim and the other progressive powers (spirits of form).

Moreover, it was always the divinely-inspired intention of Yahweh-Elohim and the other progressive celestial beings to enable human beings to be free. This would certainly have occurred without any interference from Lucifer and company. What "bright radiant Lucifer" brought to humanity was not true freedom, but an evil counterfeit. Luciferic freedom is the libertine extolment of selfishness, personal pridefulness and egocentric independence. If Lucifer is truly the "real creator and benefactor, the Father of Spiritual mankind" as H.P. Blavatsky contended, why does he continually strive to lull unsuspecting human beings into an isolated condition of dream-filled fantasy, and then to ferret them off to a bogus planet entirely under his control. Hardly the paragon of human freedom that his duped and deluded supporters so proudly extol and proclaim.

As further esoteric proof that Yahweh-Elohim is the true promoter of human freedom and not Lucifer, since the incarnation of Christ-Jesus, Yahweh-Elohim and his fellow moon-beings no longer maintain the reproductive forces of heredity, and strengthen the social-bonds of tribalism. In spiritual union with the force of divine love that has been instilled in the human soul by Christ-Jesus, Yahweh and his angels now work to promote the worldwide human family, under divine direction, and freely united by universal love for one another.

Conversely, it is Lucifer and his renegade spirits who are regressively fanning the fires of tribal and racial separation: rabid nationalism in the West and tribal warfare in the Middle East. As well, the Luciferic control of the reproductive forces of heredity has resulted in morally-disturbing DNA manipulation, animal cloning and genetically-modified foods. As Rudolf Steiner conveyed in the same lesson quoted previously (26 October 1917):

In more recent times, therefore, the spirits of light [that is, Yahweh-Elohim and the lunar-spirits] have changed their function. They now inspire human beings to develop independent ideas, feelings and impulses for freedom; they now make it their concern to establish the basis on which people can be independent individuals. And it is gradually becoming the task of the spirits who are related to the old spirits of darkness [that is, Lucifer and his renegade-spirits] to work within the blood bonds.

The function which was right in the past or, better said, belonged to the sphere of the good spirits of light, was handed over to the spirits of darkness during the last third of the nineteenth century. From this time onwards, the old impulses based on racial, tribal and national relationships, on the blood, became the domain of the spirits of darkness, who had previously been rebels in the cause of independence. They then began to instill ideas in human minds that affairs should be ordered on the basis of tribal relationships, of blood bonds. (Ibid.)

9.5 Yahweh-Elohim's Mission to Prepare the Ancient Hebrews for the Birth of the Messiah

In connection with Yahweh's wise and beneficent regulation of heredity and blood relationships in ancient times, he was also divinely tasked with preparing the Hebrew people for the incarnation of the Messiah. As biblically indicated, this preparation took many generations to achieve: fourteen generations from Abraham to King David; another fourteen from David to the Babylonian captivity; and a further fourteen from captivity to Joseph and Mary.

One can easily conclude from reading the Old Testament that preparing the ancient Hebrews was not an easy task, given that they were a characteristically stubborn and "stiff-necked" people. Nevertheless, Yahweh raised up generations of priests, prophets and kings in order to establish the strong moral foundation required for a holy nation.

One of the most significant preparations for the incarnation of the Solar-Christos as messiah was through the prophet Moses. With instruction and training from Yahweh, Moses was able to experience "I AM" consciousness for the first time in human history. This profound spiritual experience has been biblically described as God revealing to Moses—from out of a miraculous burning bush that wasn't consumed—that his holy name is "I AM."

Esoterically interpreted, the burning bush is an external projection of the blood-red, multi-branching circulatory system. From out of the elemental fire, or warmth-ether, that pulsates through the blood system of the body, Moses was able to experience his spirit-self as a reflection of God's nature. However, Moses didn't experienced his spirit-self internally; but rather, externally to himself. It was only through the incarnation of Christ-Jesus that the spirit-self was first experienced *within* the human soul. Nevertheless, Moses' divine encounter was a crucially-necessary step to prepare for the messiah.

Despite their repeated failings and set-backs, as Yahweh's "chosen people," the ancient Hebrews did eventually provide the required hereditary conditions for the incarnation of the messiah, Christ-Jesus. Sadly, many Hebrew descendents have yet to recognize Christ-Jesus as the true messiah and the saviour of mankind.

Also well worth mentioning in connection with the evolutionary unfoldment of spirit-self consciousness, is the esoteric fact that the triad of evil has continually opposed this supersensible perception. Lucifer, for example, strives to conceal any human awareness of spirit-self behind an illusory, cosmic façade of hallucinatory imagery. Ahriman, on the other hand, strives to conceal spirit-self perception from humanity beneath a perceptual veil of physical matter. As for Sorath, his strategy has always been to use vicious, blood-stained violence whenever he can in an attempt to destroy those who promote spirit-self perception. Not surprisingly then, it was Sorathic impulses that drove King Herod to slaughter innocent children in an unsuccessful attempt to murder the infant Jesus; and it was Sorathic impulses that incited the Hebrew high-priest Caiaphas to have the Romans brutally crucify the innocent Christ-Jesus.

9.6 Yahweh-Elohim as the Principal Embodiment of the Holy Mother-Spirit for the Third Hierarchy

The popular understanding of Yahweh-Elohim has very much been coloured by his Old Testament persona as a strict and authoritarian, masculine deity. While this is certainly an aspect of his historical mission, Yahweh-Elohim also has a gentler and deeper feminine nature that is often unacknowledged, except in mythology. As the planetary-spirit of the moon, he is often portrayed as a moon-goddess, rather than as a moon-god, in mythology. In Roman mythology, for example, he was known as Luna and Diana. In Greek mythology, he was known as Selene and Artemis.

The masculine and feminine duality to the nature of Yahweh-Elohim is also reflected in a variation of his name—"Yod-Eva"—where Yod is his masculine side, and Eva or Eve is his feminine side.

Also noteworthy when considering Yahweh-Elohim, in accordance with the universal principle of triplicity,[41] within the Life of the Universe (the Logos-Word), there are three main divisions of advanced beings; and within each main division, there are three sub-divisions as well. The hierarchic division closest to mankind, known as the Third Hierarchy, is comprised of: (1) angels (or moon-spirits), (2) archangels (or sun-spirits), and (3) archai (or time-spirits).

As the foremost initiate-leader of the angelic moon-spirits, Yahweh-Elohim is the principal embodiment and representative of the Holy Mother-Spirit within the Third Hierarchy (please refer to Figure 5 on page 99). Also in this connection, the preeminent initiate-leader of the archaic time-spirits, Chronos-Aeon, is the principal embodiment and representative of the Heavenly Father within the Third Hierarchy (and is therefore also known as "Father Time"). And, of course, the exalted initiate-leader of the archangelic sun-spirits, the Solar-Christos, is the principal embodiment and representative of the Eternal Son within the Third Hierarchy.

CHAPTER 10

CELESTIAL BENEFACTORS OF MANKIND: MICHAEL THE ARCHAI

10.1 St. Michael: The Great Opponent of the Dragon of Evil

WHILE THERE ARE certainly numerous other celestial benefactors of mankind that are worthy of mention and discussion, in order to positively counterbalance the three main perpetrators of evil that have been identified in this discourse, only a third especially-noteworthy benefactor will be extolled here. That celestial advocate is, of course, Michael the Archai.

Throughout the pre-Christian age of Yahweh-Elohim, and continuing into the age of Christ-Jesus, Michael's primary contribution to earth evolution has been his divinely-assigned role as mankind's preeminent protector and defender against evil. In this capacity, he has fought and won numerous wars in heaven, and prevailed against many different dragons of evil.

Most recently, from 1841 to 1879, Michael and his faithful

companions were victorious in heaven over a dragon of accumulated materialism wielded by Mammon[42] and a dark horde of Ahrimanic demons. In consequence, the Ahrimanic demons were expelled from heaven and cast down to the earth. While this expulsion beneficially purified the heavenly realm, it unfortunately resulted in Ahrimanic demons invisibly assailing unsuspecting human beings on earth. Thankfully, ever the reliable protector, Michael also sacrificially descended to the earth in order to shield mankind from this newly-imposed evil threat.[43]

10.2 Michael as Mankind's Guardian of Spiritual Truth

As Rudolf Steiner has well remarked: "Michael is the spirit who works, in the most eminent sense, with the *freedom* of man. Michael will always do what is necessary. You must not believe that Michael fails to do the right thing" (Ibid.). Once again, here is clear esoteric confirmation that true human freedom was not something "bestowed" by Lucifer; but instead, a hard-fought evolutionary struggle that has been won for mankind by benevolent celestial beings such as Michael the Archai.

In service to humanity, Michael continues to guard and protect intellectual access to spiritual truth. For this reason, he is also esoterically titled, the "regent of cosmic intelligence." Imaginatively, then, the sword that Michael wields against the dragon of darkness is the sword of spiritual truth.

The super-earthly battle that was won by Michael and his hosts in 1879 was against Ahrimanic spirits who were attempting to prevent human beings from cognitively accessing the spiritual world. Since the mid-nineteenth century, the sudden torrent of materialistic-minded souls into the after-death region closest to the earth began to seriously darken and obstruct perception and comprehension of the spiritual world. Added to this, the Ahrimanic spirits saw an opportunity of using the choking cloud of dark materialistic miasma to permanently block the future development of spirit-perception and spirit-knowledge.

Michael's victory meant that he was able to dispel the etheric "fog of Ahrimanic materialism" that was threatening evolution on earth, and thereby provide humanity with clear and unhindered intellectual access to the spirit world. Unfortunately, even though mankind in its long history has never had clearer access to spirit-knowledge and to spirit-understanding than it does since Michael's victory in 1879, the Ahrimanic spirits cast to the earth are better able to infect human thinking with their anti-spirit thoughts. In other words, the danger still exists that even though human beings now have better access to spiritual truth, if they Ahrimanically believe that a spiritual world doesn't exist, then they obviously won't bother to seek that newly-available truth.

10.3 Spiritual Science as a Modern-Day Initiative of Michael

According to the clairvoyant research of Rudolf Steiner, mankind's cognitive capacity of intellectual thinking has very much been influenced and molded by Luciferic intrusion. Not surprisingly, the ability to internally generate free and independent abstract ideas that are not necessarily connected to outer reality would very much assist Lucifer in directing human attention away from the earth.

This Luciferic involvement in shaping and developing the human intellect was largely the result of two noteworthy events. One of these events was a previous war in heaven where rebellious Luciferic spirits were cast down to earth by Michael and his hosts. Once cast to the earth, these Luciferic spirits turned their attention to human thinking; and in particular, to stimulating intellectual abstraction.

The other noteworthy event, of course, was the physical incarnation of Lucifer in ancient China around 3000 BC. During this incarnation, Lucifer developed the human capacity to actively grasp super-earthly (mystery) knowledge through the powers of the intellect; rather than simply receiving it passively through revelation. Mystery knowledge that had previously been conveyed entirely through symbolic imagery, could now be comprehended and conveyed by using intellectual concepts.

Unfortunately, but not unpredictably, the Luciferically-fashioned intellect was not intended to lead mankind towards spiritual truth; but instead, to mystical fantasy and illusion. Moreover, the objectivity required for intellectual thinking drove a psychic wedge between the individual and the surrounding spiritual world. With increased spiritual separation, human attention began to be directed more and more to the physical, material world instead.

This increased preoccupation with the physical world provided the Ahrimanic spirits who were cast down to earth in 1879 with an opportunity to densify and constrict superphysical intellectual thinking into becoming more of a brain-based chemical activity instead. To prevent this from occurring, Michael himself—the great defender of spiritual truth—descended to the earth as well. In order to counteract the Luciferic and Ahrimanic attempts to completely hijack the human intellect, Michael inspired the establishment of anthroposophical spiritual science through Rudolf Steiner at the beginning of the twentieth century.

Through spiritual science, Michael has provided humanity with the opportunity and the means to "spiritualize" the human intellect; that is, to properly re-direct intellectual thinking to the now-accessible spiritual world; together with the capacity to comprehend and convey spiritual knowledge in the form of clear intellectual concepts.

10.4 Michael as the New Herald and Guardian of the Etheric Christ-Jesus

The Ahrimanic uprising that took place between 1841 and 1879 was not just a general assault on the human capacity to intellectually access the spiritual world, but it was also a targeted assassination attempt on the etheric life of Christ-Jesus in the realm of Shambhala. Since the combined forces of evil had failed to sever mankind's connection to the Solar-Christos during the Graeco-Roman era by brutally crucifying the *physical* body of Jesus-Immanuel, they mounted a similar attack on the *etheric* body of Jesus-Immanuel during the modern era.

By permanently shadowing and obscuring Jesus-Immanuel's conscious awareness of the indwelling Solar-Christos with a darkening layer of etheric miasma, the powers of evil were intending to sever human access to the spiritual world and to spiritual truth. Alarmingly, a death-like diminishment of consciousness did actually occur for a short length of time; and it initially appeared that Jesus-Immanuel had lost consciousness of the indwelling Solar-Christos, and of his higher God-self.

Thankfully, with the defensive protection of Michael and his hosts, the suffocating cloud of etheric materialism was successfully dispelled, and the horde of Ahrimanic assassins were cast down to earth. Similar to the stupendous after-death events of the crucifixion on Golgotha, there occurred a triumphant "resurrection" following the failed assassination in Shambhala. In this case, however, it was not so much a resurrection of the body, but a resurrection of "spirit-consciousness."

Michael's victory over the death-dealing Ahrimanic forces

in 1879, not only re-established and strengthened humanity's connection to Christ-Jesus and to the entire spiritual world, but it also cleared the way for Christ-Jesus to begin to etherically appear on earth—beginning in 1933. This new appearance of Christ-Jesus in the etheric form of an angel is what spiritual science understands as the "Second Coming." Moreover, without the spiritual science inspired by Michael, it would not be possible for human beings to knowingly experience and to intellectually understand this profound second coming of Christ-Jesus.

It's also important for esotericists to recall at this point, that similar to the super-earthly battle that occurred in the nineteenth century, Michael continues to defeat the Ahrimanic dragon of materialism; and thereby prepare the way for the earthly descent of Christ-Jesus—each and every year.

As the new planetary-spirit of the earth, Christ-Jesus is conjoined to the seasonal "inbreathing" and "outbreathing" of planetary consciousness. During each summer season, the planetary consciousness of Christ-Jesus expands outwardly into the vast reaches of outer space; thereby merging for a brief but glorious time with the empyrean ocean of cosmic consciousness. Then, at the zenith-point of the summer solstice, the reinvigorated planetary consciousness of Christ-Jesus rhythmically returns to the earth.

During the summer months, however, the surrounding planetary atmosphere becomes "sulphurized"; that is, permeated with a global tincture of vaporous sulphur. With the gradual, volcanic escape of noxious sulphuric gases into the atmosphere, the subterranean Ahrimanic spirits are able to rise up out of the earth during the late summer season. To clairvoyant perception ("imaginative consciousness"), these Ahrimanic spirits collectively assume the astral form of a "fire-breathing" dragon—a monstrous, serpentine creature that "feeds" on combustible sulphur in the air.

During the autumnal season, in order to purify and safeguard the earth's atmosphere for the seasonal return of the planetary consciousness of Christ-Jesus, Michael cosmically showers the earth with meteoric iron; thereby re-banishing the Ahrimanic dragon to its underground lair for another season.[44] In the pre-Christian age, as the archangelic folk-spirit of the ancient Hebrews, Michael faithfully assisted Yahweh-Elohim to prepare and sanctify the way for the messiah's incarnation. Now, in the Christian age, Michael has advanced to the level of a time-spirit (archai); and as the current "spirit of the age," he faithfully acts as the herald and guardian of the etheric Christ-Jesus.

10.5 The Power of Michael Casts Out Ahrimanic Fear, Hatred and Anxiety from Within the Human Body

Consistent with the other great benefactors of mankind (as well as the principal perpetrators of evil), Michael not only acts macrocosmically in his mission for humanity, but his protective range of influence also extends microcosmically to within the human being as well.

The seasonal battle that Michael wages on a planetary level with the Ahrimanic dragon, simultaneously occurs on a physiological level within each human being. During the summer season, the tincture of sulphur that also permeates the human bloodstream, undergoes a subtle process of etheric combustion. As a result, the human form begins to supersensibly glow with an internal astral light. Unfortunately, this sulphuric astral glow attracts Ahrimanic spirits—like moths to a flame—who then collectively coil around the heart in a serpentine, dragon-like form.

The subconscious presence of this microcosmic dragon of evil incites the lower animal nature to rise up into awareness as feelings of fear, hate and anxiety. Similar to what occurs on a planetary level, this internal Ahrimanic dragon is dispelled by a sparkling shower of minute iron particles that are held within the red blood cells. This blood-iron is physiologically wielded like a purifying sword by Michael, in a manner similar to his cosmic shower of meteoric iron in the earth's atmosphere. This amazing but little-known process was described in much clearer detail by Rudolf Steiner in a lecture given on 05 October 1923 entitled "The Michael Imagination." The following is a brief excerpt from that lecture:

> And this majestic display in cosmic space, when the August meteor showers stream down into the human shining in the astral light, has its counterpart—so gentle and apparently so small—in a change that occurs in the human blood. This human blood ... is rayed through by the force which is carried as iron into the blood and wages war there on anxiety, fear and hate. The processes which are set going in every blood-corpuscle when the force of iron shoots into it are the same, on a minute human scale, as those which take place when meteors fall in a shining stream through the air. This permeation of human blood by the anxiety-dispelling force of iron is a meteoric activity. The effect of the raying in of the iron is to drive fear and anxiety out of the blood. (Published in *The Four Seasons and the Archangels*; 1996)

10.6 Michael: Guardian Knight of the Universal Woman

What is referred to in spiritual science as "cosmic intelligence" is a reflection within the created universe of divine wisdom. Divine wisdom is personified within the trinitarian nature of God as the Holy Mother. Cosmic intelligence, then, is a reflection of the Holy Mother; and is also esoterically referred to as the "universal feminine principle" of the Logos-Word (please refer to Chapter subsection 7.4 if necessary).

As the divinely-appointed protector of mankind's access to cosmic intelligence, Michael is therefore also correctly understood to be the great defender of the "universal woman." This responsibility has been symbolically portrayed in The Revelation to John, Chapter 12:

> And a great portent appeared in heaven, a woman clothed with the sun, with the moon under her feet, and on her head a crown of twelve stars ... And another portent appeared in heaven; behold, a great red dragon, with seven heads and ten horns, and seven diadems upon his heads. His tail swept down a third of the stars of heaven, and cast them to the earth. And the dragon stood before the woman who was about to bear a child, that he might devour her child when she brought it forth ... Now war arose in heaven, Michael and his angels fighting against the dragon; and the dragon and his angels fought, but they were defeated and there was no longer any place for them in heaven. And the great dragon was thrown down, that ancient serpent, who is called the Devil and Satan, the deceiver of the whole world—he was thrown down to the earth, and his angels were thrown down with him.

The "woman clothed with the sun" can also be correctly seen as a symbol for Blessed Mary (the mother of Jesus) and for the Church (as the mystical body of Christ), since they both especially embody the Holy Spirit-Mother. As the great defender of cosmic intelligence, then, Michael is also the great cosmic protector of Blessed Mary and the Christian Church.

It's quite obvious that Michael's role as the gallant protector of the "universal woman" served as the heavenly inspiration for chivalrous Medieval knights to pledge their lives in serving "Our Lady."

CONCLUSION:

MOVING POSITIVELY INTO THE FUTURE

C.1 Salvation From Supernatural Evil is a Free-Will Choice

IT SHOULD BE esoterically obvious from all that has been written thus far, that without the benevolent assistance of many highly-advanced celestial beings mankind would become easy prey for supernatural evil. The perpetrators of supernatural evil are far too powerful, and far too clever, for unassisted human beings to overcome on our own.

Furthermore, even though Christ-Jesus has successfully triumphed over Lucifer, Ahriman and Sorath, he does not impose his own success on the rest of humanity. Instead, he freely offers his power, capacity and assistance to overcome evil for anyone who sincerely chooses. Unfortunately, many in our day have not chosen to do so. Far too many people continue to happily endorse the atheistic and materialistic world-view of empirical science. Far too many people continue to be mesmerized by the hedonistic technology of secular society. Far too many people continue to evade spiritual reality with escapist movies, books, games, drugs, sports and music. The discerning observer of modern life cannot help but painfully conclude that supernatural evil will continue to plague somnolent humanity for the foreseeable future.

C.2 The Tragic Irony of Evil: Opposing God is Opposing Our Own True Self

It is still somewhat of a cosmic mystery to understand why otherwise highly-advanced beings such as Lucifer, Ahriman and Sorath willingly choose to engage in evil; that is, freely choose to act contrary to God. The undeniable spiritual fact is that all sentient beings are children of God; and therefore the divine spirit is mirrored in every self-conscious being. Furthermore, the highest self of all self-conscious beings—holy and evil—is their God-self, their true eternal life and reality.

Moreover, according to logical reasoning, the triune God is perfectly free and infinitely happy. So it also logically follows that for all created beings—including the supernatural perpetrators of evil—the highest freedom and happiness can only come from spiritual union with God.

So, when Lucifer, Ahriman or Sorath flee from the divine light of truth and the divine warmth of love, they are truly and tragically fleeing from their own highest spiritual selves. Separating from God through sin is in fact separating from who they are in reality. Moreover, running from this spiritual fact does in no way change it. Only by embracing the truth of their ultimate being, in sincere humility and gratitude, is there lasting salvation from a sorrowful life of evil.

C.3 Divine Love is the Best Way of Dealing with Evil

I John 4:18 states in part that "perfect love casts out fear." What is also implied with this spiritual truth is that "perfect (divine) love casts out evil." After examining in some detail the nature, genesis and supernatural perpetration of evil, as well as the celestial beings who benefit humanity and oppose evil, what comes into clear intellectual focus is the convincing conclusion that the best way of dealing with evil is through divine love.

The foremost exemplar of divine love in all of human history is, of course, our saviour Christ-Jesus. Through his life on earth, his gospel teachings and his resurrected presence in the Church, Christ-Jesus has provided mankind with a sure path of holiness that will overcome evil and lead directly to God. Our Saviour has taught and demonstrated that we are not to hate, revile or despise the evil enemies of mankind; but instead, to love them. This, of course, does not mean that we are to befriend our supernatural enemies and overlook their evil ways; but rather, to remind ourselves that they too are children of God, albeit lost and mistaken. Hopefully, one day, they will realize the error of their evil ways, and turn back to their true home in God.

Furthermore, regarding the supernatural perpetrators of evil with infinite compassion does not mean that the forces of holiness do nothing about evil in their midst. Since all persons under unwarranted attack have a right to appropriate self-defense, the benevolent celestial beings have every right to resist, repel, disable, disarm, deactivate, neutralize, subdue, contain, incarcerate and imprison the perpetrators of evil who intend to do others (and themselves) harm. Self-defense, in this case however, is not undertaken in a spirit of revenge or retaliation; but in the spirit of Michael—the spirit of divine justice, fairness and doing what is morally right in the eyes of God.

Since all sentient beings possess the divine gift of free-will, perpetrators of evil cannot be forced against their will to be holy. The free-will decision to turn from evil to holiness is what is understood as "redemption." The will to do evil can only be overcome and reversed through a personal act of redemption. The material or superphysical manifestations of evil, however, can be transformed or transmuted. For example, by raising the vibratory level of etheric debasements, such as electricity and magnetism, these manifestations of evil can be transmuted back into light and chemical ether, for the positive benefit of earthly evolution.

Furthermore, much of modern technology—such as computers, robotics, genetic modification and automation—is a "double-edged sword"; it can be used for the benefit of mankind, or for earthly destruction. Modern technology, then, must be increasingly wrested from the control of Ahrimanic spirits and put into the hands of Michael and other Christ-imbued beings. Similarly, the various forms of artistic expression—such as filmmaking, theatre, painting, sculpture, computer graphics and music—must increasingly be directed away from Luciferic fantasy and illusion; and instead, directed towards the uplifting expression of true spiritual beauty.

In summary, by assisting our planetary-spirit, Christ-Jesus, with the transmutation and transformation of the "old" universe into the "new heaven and the new earth," the supernatural perpetrators of evil will be increasingly surrounded by the light of divine truth and the warmth of divine love. Consequently, this will increasingly limit the dark places they can hide; and more importantly, it will increasingly limit their ability to debase matter, energy and mind to use as weapons in their arsenal of evil. In time, by increasingly protecting ourselves, and them, in a cosmic cocoon of holiness, this will incite the larvae of evil to metamorphose into the prodigal butterflies of spiritual redemption.

No doubt, transforming the universe to this supernal degree of divine love will take many aeons to accomplish; but after all, this is the divine plan of creation—the destiny of the Logos-Word as the image and likeness of God.

NOTES

CHAPTER 3

1. Gnosticism was a diverse and syncretistic, pre-Christian philosophical and religious movement. Gnosticism was characterized by wildly-novel and strangely-exotic ideas regarding God, the universe, mankind and Christ-Jesus. Many of these extravagant notions were considered to be heretical by the early Christian Church.
2. The assertion that "good" is a transcendent aspect of God's nature is biblically supported by Christ-Jesus in the gospel of Matthew (10:18), which states: "And Jesus said to him, 'Why do you call me good? No one is good but God alone.'"
3. As conveyed biblically: "So God created man in his own image, in the image of God he created him; male and female he created them" (Gen 1:27).
4. This was the seductive lie that was used on nascent humanity by the devilish serpent in primordial paradise: "By disobeying God's commandment (by doing evil), you will be free like God to know good and evil."

NOTES

CHAPTER 4

5. As stated by Rudolf Steiner in a lecture given on 24 August 1910 entitled "Stages of Human Development up to the Sixth Day of Creation":

   > Paradise was not situated upon earthly soil, that it was lifted above the earth, was so to say in the heights of the clouds, and that while man lived in Paradise he remained a being of warmth and air. At that time man did not actually walk about the earth on two legs; that is a materialistic fantasy ... we have to think of man as a being belonging not to the ground, but to the periphery of the earth.
   >
   > Thus the soul-spiritual man hovers in the periphery of the developing earth. He is as it were within the substance of the several spiritual Beings. So far he has no independent existence. It is as if he were being fashioned as an organ within the Elohim, the Archai and so on—as though he were in their bodies as part of them. (Published in *Genesis: Secrets of the Bible Story of Creation*; 1959)

6. According to spiritual science, independent soul-substance was freely gifted to our human ancestors by a class of advanced superphysical beings known as the "spirits of form" or "elohim" (please refer to Figure 1 on page 31). It is also maintained that the being referred to in the Old Testament as Yahweh was one of the elohim, which helps to explain the biblical statement: "[T]hen the LORD God [Yahweh-Elohim] formed man of dust from the ground, and breathed into his nostrils the breath of life; and man became a living being" (Gen 2:7).

7. Spiritual science has clairvoyantly identified two additional intermediary form-bodies that lie between the physical body and the ego-bearing soul. These form-

bodies are superphysical and interpenetrate the physical body and soul. The first of these form-bodies, known as the "etheric body," is a subtle vehicle for the various life forces that maintain the form and function of the physical body. The second of these form-bodies, known as the "astral body," is an even subtler vehicle that enables sense perception, sensation, rudimentary feeling and desire. (For more detailed information, please refer to Rudolf Steiner's book *Theosophy*; 1994)

8. As described by Rudolf Steiner in a lecture given on 20 March 1916 entitled "The Weaving and Living Activity of the Human Etheric Bodies":

> The serpent is Lucifer ... Lucifer can only be perceived through the inner eye ... Lucifer should be imagined as spiritual science is able to represent him ... If we go back into evolution, if we were to perceive Lucifer through our inner power of vision, we would see him in the form which he had upon the [Ancient] Moon [Period of planetary evolution], when he was preparing the earthly human head ... and attached to it was a human spine, a spinal cord, that may be imagined in the form of a serpent's body ... This would be a kind of picture of Lucifer.

This "picture of Lucifer" has been quite accurately portrayed by William Blake (1757–1827) in his painting "The Great Red Dragon and the Woman Clothed with the Sun" (1805–1810). This is the painting that has been creatively used by the author for the front cover design of this publication.

9. In Greek mythology, Prometheus was a god who stole fire from Mt. Olympus for the benefit of mankind. As punishment, Zeus chained him to a rock in the Caucasus Mountains where he was daily tormented by an eagle until being freed by Hercules.

10. As Rudolf Steiner conveyed in a lecture given on 21 August 1911 entitled "Wonders of the World":

> Lucifer himself takes part in Earth evolution with the perpetual longing within him for his true home, for the star Venus outside in the cosmos. That is the salient feature of the Luciferic nature seen from the cosmic aspect. Clairvoyant consciousness comes to know just what the star of Venus is by entering into the soul of Lucifer, thus experiencing from the Earth Lucifer's tragic longing, like a wonderful cosmic nostalgia, for the star Phosphorus, Lucifer or Venus.

11. Though not identical to the Lemurian continent of spiritual science, geologic science has postulated a similar supercontinent in the southern hemisphere, named Gondwanaland, that supposedly existed about 450 million years ago during the Ordovician Period.

12. The gradual condensation of prehistoric fire-mist and the watery submergence of Atlantis is figuratively portrayed in Genesis as the "great flood of Noah":

> "[N]ever again shall all flesh be cut off by the waters of a flood, and never again shall there be a flood to destroy the earth." And God said, "This is the sign of the covenant which I make between me and you and every living creature that is with you, for all future generations: I set my [rain]bow in the cloud, and it shall be a sign of the covenant between me and the earth." (Gen 9:11–13)

13. Concerning the future possibility of Lucifer forever ending his evil use of free-will, statements made by Rudolf Steiner in a lecture given on 22 November 1914 and later published in *The Balance in the World and Man: Lucifer and Ahriman* (1977), give reason for optimism:

> Thus we are truly, in a certain connection, redeemers

of Lucifer. When we begin to be able to love our duty, then the moment has come when we can help towards the redemption and release of the Luciferic powers; we set free the Lucifer forces which are held in us as by a charm, and lead them forth to fight with Ahriman. We release the imprisoned Lucifer (imprisoned in self-love) when we learn to love our duty.

CHAPTER 5

14. In the words of Rudolf Steiner that were given in a lecture on 15 November 1919:

   We have only to remember that it is the endeavour of the Ahrimanic powers to reduce the earth to a state of complete rigidification. Their victory would be won if they succeeded in bringing earth, water and air into this rigidified state. (Published in *The Influences of Lucifer and Ahriman*, 1995)

15. According to spiritual-scientific clairvoyant research, pathological bacteria (bacilli) were originally generated by Ahrimanic beings who were cast down to earth after a prehistoric war in heaven. As described by Rudolf Steiner in a lecture given on 14 October 1917 entitled "The Battle Between Michael and the 'Dragon'":

   After one of these battles, for example, the crowd of ahrimanic spirits populated the earth with the earthly life-forms which the medical profession now calls bacilli. Everything which has the power to act as a bacillus, everything in which bacilli are involved, is the result of crowds of ahrimanic spirits being cast down from heaven to earth at a time when the dragon [Ahriman] had been overcome. (Published in *The Fall*

NOTES

of the Spirits of Darkness; 1996) Presumable, viruses are also Ahrimanic formulations since they are equally pathogenic and have "the power to act as a bacillus."

16. For a penetrating insight and analysis into the socially-destructive economic self-interest of modern-day corporations, an outstanding book on the subject is by legal theorist Joel Bakan, entitled *The Corporation: The Pathological Pursuit of Profit and Power* (2005).

17. Anthroposophist Bernard Lievegoed (1905–1992), in his book *The Battle for the Soul* (1993), made the following statement: "But Rudolf Steiner added that Ahriman will do everything in his power to accelerate this incarnation to the year 1998."

18. As clearly indicated by Rudolf Steiner: "... the bodily existence of a human individuality in whom Ahriman can incarnate, will become possible and inevitable" (from a lecture given on 2 November 1919, and published in *The Influences of Lucifer and Ahriman*; 1995).

CHAPTER 6

19. The volcanic destruction of Lemuria through the misuse of human will was pointed out by Rudolf Steiner in a lecture given on 12 June 1906 entitled "Earthquakes, Volcanoes and the Will of Man":

> Underneath the solid earth there are a large number of subterranean spaces which communicate to the sixth layer, that of fire. This element of the fire-earth is intimately connected with the human will. It is this element which has produced the tremendous eruptions that brought the Lemurian epoch to an end. At that time the forces which nourish the human will

went through a trial which unleashed the fire catastrophe that destroyed the Lemurian continent. In the course of evolution this sixth layer receded more and more toward the center and as a result volcanic eruptions became less frequent. And yet they are still produced as a result of the human will which, when it is evil and chaotic, magnetically acts on this layer and disrupts it. Nevertheless, when the human will is devoid of egoism, it is able to appease this fire. Materialistic periods are mostly accompanied and followed by natural cataclysms, earthquakes, etc. Growing powers of evolution are the only alchemy capable of transforming, little by little, the organism and the soul of the earth. (Published in *An Esoteric Cosmology*; 2013)

20. As described by Rudolf Steiner in a lecture given on 01 January 1909 entitled "Mephistopheles and Earthquakes":

> [I]n Atlantean times the seminal forces in plant and animal were still at man's command and could be drawn forth just as the forces used in the form of steam for propelling machines can be extracted from mineral coal to-day. I have told you that when these forces are drawn forth they are connected in a mysterious way with the nature-forces in wind, weather and the like; and if applied by man for purposes running counter to the divine purposes, these nature-forces are called into action against him.
>
> Here lies the cause of the Atlantean flood and of the devastation wrought by the powers of nature which led to the disappearance of the whole continent of Atlantis. But even before that time, man had lost command over the forces of fire and the power to ally them with certain mysterious forces of the earth. Power over the forces of fire and earth in a certain

combination had already been withdrawn from man. (Published in *The Deed of Christ and the Opposing Spiritual Powers*; 1976)

21. This assertion is also supported by the akashic research of spiritual science, as conveyed by Rudolf Steiner in a lecture given on 01 January 1909, entitled "Mephistopheles and Earthquakes":

> Nearly every ancient civilization—the Indian, the Persian, the Egyptian, the Greco-Latin—had its period of decadence; so too the Mysteries, when the Mystery-traditions were no longer preserved in their purity. During these periods many of those who were either pupils of the Initiates but unable to remain at their level or men to whom the secrets of the Mysteries had been unlawfully betrayed, had fallen into perverse and evil paths. Centers of black magic and its forces originated from these influences and have persisted to this day. (Published in *The Deed of Christ and the Opposing Spiritual Powers*; 1976)

22. This quotation is from a lecture given by Rudolf Steiner on 01 September 1910, and published in *According to Matthew: The Gospel of Christ's Humanity* (2003).
23. As described by Rudolf Steiner in a lecture given on 01 January 1909 entitled "Mephistopheles and Earthquakes":

> The practice of black magic by the descendants of the Atlanteans in ancient Persia would still have been effective had not the teachings of Zarathustra revealed how Ahriman, as an opposing power, ensnares man and clouds his vision of the spiritual reality behind the world of sense. (Published in *The Deed of Christ and the Opposing Spiritual Powers*; 1976)

24. The later Mexican Aztecs (whose name derives from "the people from Aztlán"—that is, Atlantis) who continued the

cruel and bloody practices of black-magic, corrupted the benevolent sun-being Vitzliputzli into a blood-thirsty sun-demon named "Huitzilopochtli" (Sorath), who required regular human sacrifices to continue shining.

25. Even though the genocidal extermination of European Jews was not used by the Nazi hierarchy as a means to increase their personal black-magical power, Sorath was able to illicitly extract a superabundance of life-ether from the millions of murdered victims, and then compress and degrade it into a vast amount of subterranean nuclear force.

26. Rudolf Steiner similarly touched on the "law of twelve" in a lecture given on 22 January 1914:

> As the sun apparently passes through the Zodiac, and as other planets apparently do the same, so it is possible for the human soul to pass through a mental circle which embraces twelve world-pictures. Indeed, one can even bring the characteristics of these pictures into connection with the individual signs of the Zodiac, and this is in no wise arbitrary, for between the individual signs of the Zodiac and the Earth there really is a connection similar to that between the twelve world-outlooks and the human soul. (Published in *Human and Cosmic Thought*; 2015)

27. As the new planetary-spirit of the earth, Christ-Jesus also takes part in the seasonal "inbreathing" and "outbreathing" rhythm of the earth. Consequently, he descends from Shambhala to the centre of the earth at the winter solstice (December 21/22), and ascends from Shambhala to the heavenly heights at the summer solstice (June 21/22).

CHAPTER 7

28. The initial formulation of the Hermetic teachings has been traditionally attributed to Hermes Trismegistus ("thrice-great"), a highly-advanced initiate who helped establish ancient Egyptian civilization around 2000 BC. Also known in Egyptian mythology as Thoth, according to spiritual science, Hermes' prodigious talents were partially due to the fact that he mystically incorporated the preserved astral body of the ancient Persian bodhisattva, Zoroaster.

29. The understanding that thoughts are basically vortices of mental space has been familiar to Yoga philosophy since ancient times. As explained by Yogi Ramacharaka in *Raja Yoga or Mental Development* (1934):

> Mind-substance in Sanskrit is called *"Chitta,"* and a wave in the *Chitta* (which wave is the combination of Mind and Energy) is called *"Vritta,"* which is akin to what we call a "thought." In other words it is "mind in action," whereas *Chitta* is "mind in repose." *Vritta*, when literally translated means "a whirlpool or eddy in the mind," which is exactly what a thought really is.

30. A very succinct understanding of spirit has been given by Yogi Ramacharaka in *Lessons in Gnani Yoga: The Yoga of Wisdom* (1934):

> Mind as we know it, as well as Matter and Energy, is held by the highest occult teachers to be but an appearance and a relativity of something far more fundamental and enduring, and we are compelled to fall back upon that old term which wise men have used in order to describe that Something Else that lies back of, and under, Matter, Energy and Mind—and that word is "Spirit."
>
> We cannot tell just what is meant by the word "Spirit," for we have nothing with which to describe

it. But we can think of it as meaning the "essence" of Life and Being—the Reality underlying Universal Life.

31. A divine Trinity of Heavenly Father, Holy Mother and Eternal Son would appear to differ from the conventional theology of Father, Son and Holy Spirit. However, referring to the Holy Spirit as "he" in the Bible is mainly due to the fact that the Latin word for spirit is "spiritus," which is a masculine term. In the original Hebrew writings, the word for spirit is "ruach," which is a feminine term; and in later Greek translations, spirit is "pneuma," which is a neutral term.

    The translator of the Greek and Hebrew scriptures into the Latin Vulgate, St. Jerome (347–420), similarly remarked:

    > In the Gospel of the Hebrews that the Nazarenes read it says, "Just now my mother, the Holy Spirit, took me." Now no one should be offended by this, because 'spirit' in Hebrew is feminine, while in our [Latin] language it is masculine and in the Greek it is neuter. In divinity, however, there is no gender. (*Jerome's Commentary on Isaiah II*)

32. For a deeper and more detailed esoteric discourse on the nature of God, the divine Trinity and the creation of the universe, the interested reader is directed to one of this author's prior publications, entitled: *The Divine Trinity, the Logos-Word and Creation* (2015), which is available from Amazon.com.

33. Rudolf Steiner in a lecture given on 22 March 1909 and later published in *The Deed of Christ and the Opposing Spiritual Powers: Lucifer, Ahriman, Asuras* (1977), also drew a connection between Lucifer and the Holy Spirit:

    > This "Holy Spirit" is none other than the Lucifer-Spirit, resurrected now in higher, purer glory—the

Spirit of independent understanding, wisdom-inwoven. Christ Himself foretold that this Spirit would come to men after Him ... The torch of the resurrected Lucifer, of the Lucifer now *transformed into the good*, blazons the way for Christ. Lucifer is the *bearer* of the Light—Christ *is* the Light!

Of course, it is crucially important not to misinterpret what is being said here. Lucifer is certainly not the divine person of the Holy Spirit. What Rudolf Steiner has indicated is the hopeful prediction that at some time in the future, Lucifer will renounce his evil ways and begin to assist, rather than oppose, the Solar-Christos. If and when he does, Lucifer could beneficially embody the wisdom of the Holy Spirit, instead of corrupting it.

But as things exist now, Lucifer continues to be a formidable enemy of mankind, and is certainly no friend of the great sun-spirit, Christ.

CHAPTER 8

34. For a much more detailed esoteric examination of the world-altering after-death journey and events undertaken by Christ-Jesus, the interested reader is referred to a previous publication by this author, entitled *The Star of Higher Knowledge: The Five Guiding Mysteries of Esoteric Christianity* (2015). The book is available to order from Amazon.com.
35. One excellent example of the ubiquitous presence of Luciferic evil in the world is electricity. Esoterically understood, electricity is sunlight that has been congealed and densified by Lucifer. If one wished to avoid Lucifer entirely, then one would have to avoid any contact with electrical technology. Considering how dependent modern civilization is on the use of electricity, totally

avoiding it (and thereby Lucifer) is next to impossible.

36. It's important to keep this understanding in mind when reading certain comments by Rudolf Steiner, such as in a lecture given on 20 November 1914, which stated: "This indicates to us that in their rightfully allotted place, Lucifer and Ahriman work beneficially; in their wrongful place—there they are injurious" (published in *The Balance in the World and Man: Lucifer and Ahriman*; 1977).

Therefore, even when the evil tendencies of Lucifer and Ahriman are forcibly contained within benevolent boundaries, this does not transform them into benevolent beings. They are still malevolent beings who have been forcibly prevented from doing injury to mankind

37. The karmic consequences of misusing the high-vibrational subtle forces of nature are well described in *The Kybalion* (2013):

> But this may be said here, that those who have attained high spiritual powers and have misused them, have a terrible fate in store for them, and the swing of the pendulum of Rhythm will inevitably swing them back to the furthest extreme of Material existence, from which point they must retrace their steps Spiritward, along the weary rounds of The Path, but always with the added torture of having always with them a lingering memory of the heights from which they fell owing to their evil actions. The legends of the Fallen Angels have a basis in actual facts, as all advanced occultists know. The striving for selfish power on the Spiritual Planes inevitably results in the selfish soul losing its spiritual balance and falling back as far as it had previously risen. But to even such a soul, the opportunity of a return is given—and such souls make the return journey, paying the terrible penalty according to the invariable Law.

38. The association of maternal forces (such as heredity and reproduction) with the archangel Gabriel was well-described by Rudolf Steiner in a lecture given on 19 July 1924 entitled "From the Gabriel to the Michael Age":

> Gabriel rules over the whole realm of the physical forces of heredity within humanity. He is the supersensible Spirit who is connected essentially with the sequence of the generations, who is—if I may put it so—the great Guardian Spirit of the mothers who bring children into the world. Gabriel has to do with births, with the embryonic development of the human being. The forces of Gabriel work in the *spiritual* processes underlying the physical process of propagation. (Published in *The Archangel Michael: His Mission and Ours*; 1994)

39. As highly-advanced esotericists, the Rosicrucians are also well acquainted with utilizing the principle of polarity, as indicated from the following written material:

> In ... consideration of the Principle of Polarity ... the art of which consists in finding the Centre between the Two Extremes, and thus maintaining a Poise and Balance which is undisturbed by any mental or emotional storm.
>
> Poise is Power. Poise results from Balance. Balance is secured by adjusting and maintaining the Centre between the Poles of the Pairs of Opposites. By Balanced Poise the Master neutralizes Polarity and Rhythm, by resolving them into Unity. In the Heart of the Storm is Peace. In the Centre of Life there is Poise and Power. Seek it ever, O Neophyte—for in it thou shalt find thyself. (Published in *The Secret Doctrine of the Rosicrucians*; 1949)

40. In Figure 6, the sphere within the cube diagrammatically

represents the "sphere" of divine love radiating from the spiritual union with Christ-Jesus at the centre of the soul.

CHAPTER 9

41. In connection with the universal law of triplicity, Rudolf Steiner made similar remarks in a lecture given on 21 November 1919 entitled "The Power and Mission of Michael, Necessity of the Revaluation of Many Values":

> If you consider this whole matter you will have to say to yourselves: I am only able to understand the world if I conceive of it in connection with the number three, the triad ... Those who were initiated into such secrets of the spiritual evolution of mankind have always emphasized the fact that it is only possible to understand cosmic existence into which man is placed if it is conceived of in the sense of the triad; that it cannot be understood if it is considered on the basis of any other number.

CHAPTER 10

42. According to spiritual science, Mammon is more than just the "demon of monetary greed," as he is popularly understood. In an esoteric lesson given on 05 December 1907, Rudolf Steiner stated the following:

> For occultism Mammon isn't just the god of money. He's the leader of all base, black forces. And his hosts attack men's bodies and souls to corrode and ruin them. There's a lot of talk about bacteria today, and they influence a lot of things. In future they'll increase in a terrifying way, and many human bodies will waste

NOTES

away from terrible diseases and plagues.

Moreover, as previously mentioned in Chapter 6, Mammon is one of the "twelve princes of hell" who surround Sorath and perform his evil bidding.

43. Michael's descent to the earth was described by Rudolf Steiner in a lecture given on 17 February 1917 entitled "Signs of the Times: Michael's Battle and its Reflection on Earth":

> At the beginning of the forties of the nineteenth century, when the middle of that century had not quite been reached, the Archangel Michael gradually rose from the rank of an Archangel to that of a Time Spirit. He began at that time to undergo an evolution which enabled him to work into human life not merely from the super-earthly standpoint, but directly from the standpoint of the earthly. He had to prepare himself to descend to the earth itself, to emulate, as it were, the great procedure of Christ Jesus Himself, to take his starting point here upon the earth and to be active henceforth from the point of view of the earth.

44. Michael's seasonal battle with the Ahrimanic dragon has been evocatively detailed by Rudolf Steiner in a lecture given on 05 October 1923 entitled "The Michael Imagination":

> And when in high summer, from a particular constellation, meteors fall in great showers of cosmic iron, then this cosmic iron, which carries an enormously powerful healing force, is the weapon which the gods bring to bear against Ahriman, as dragon-like he tries to coil round the shining forms of men. The force which falls on the earth in the meteoric iron is indeed a cosmic force whereby the higher gods endeavour to gain a victory over the

Ahrimanic powers, when autumn comes on. (Published in *The Four Seasons and the Archangels: Experience of the Course of the Year in Four Cosmic Imaginations*; 1996)

SELECT BIBLIOGRAPHY

(in alphabetical order)

- *Catechism of the Catholic Church* (Our Sunday Visitor, Publishing Division, 2000)

- Holy Bible, *RSV-CE* (Ignatius Press, 2006)

- H.P. Blavatsky, *Isis Unveiled* (The Theosophical Publishing House, 1972)

- H.P. Blavatsky, *The Secret Doctrine: Volume II—Anthropogenesis* (Theosophical University Press, 2011)

- Magus Incognito, *The Secret Doctrine of the Rosicrucians* (Yogi Publication Society, 1949)

- Ron MacFarlane, *The Greater Mysteries of the Divine Trinity, the Logos-Word and Creation* (Greater Mysteries Publications, 2015)

- Ron MacFarlane, *The Star of Higher Knowledge: The Five

SELECT BIBLIOGRAPHY

Guiding Mysteries of Esoteric Christianity (Greater Mysteries Publications, 2015)

- Rudolf Steiner, *According to Matthew: The Gospel of Christ's Humanity* (SteinerBooks, 2003)

- Rudolf Steiner, *An Esoteric Cosmology* (Start Publishing LLC, 2013)

- Rudolf Steiner, *Christ in Relation to Lucifer and Ahriman* (Anthroposophic Press, 1978)

- Rudolf Steiner, *Genesis: Secrets of the Bible Story of Creation* (Anthroposophical Publishing Co., 1959)

- Rudolf Steiner, *Human and Cosmic Thought* (Rudolf Steiner Press, 2015)

- Rudolf Steiner, *Inner Impulses of Human Evolution: The Mexican Mysteries and the Knights Templar* (Anthroposophic Press, 1984)

- Rudolf Steiner, *Man in the Light of Occultism, Theosophy and Philosophy* (Garber Communications, Inc., 1989)

- Rudolf Steiner, *Secrets of the Threshold* (SteinerBooks, 1987)

- Rudolf Steiner, *The Archangel Michael: His Mission and Ours* (SteinerBooks, 1994)

- Rudolf Steiner, *The Balance in the World and Man: Lucifer and Ahriman* (Steiner Book Centre, 1977)

- Rudolf Steiner, *The Book of Revelation and the Work of the Priest* (Rudolf Steiner Press, 1998)

- Rudolf Steiner, *The Deed of Christ and the Opposing Spiritual Powers* (Steiner Book Centre, 1976)

- Rudolf Steiner, *The Fall of the Spirits of Darkness* (Rudolf Steiner Press, 1996)

- Rudolf Steiner, *The Four Seasons and the Archangels: Experience of the Course of the Year in Four Cosmic Imaginations* (Rudolf Steiner Press, 1996)

- Rudolf Steiner, *The Influence of Spiritual Beings upon Man* (Literary Licensing LLC, 2011)

- Rudolf Steiner, *The Influences of Lucifer and Ahriman* (SteinerBooks, 1995)

- Rudolf Steiner, *Theosophy* (SteinerBooks, 1994)

- Rudolf Steiner, *The Reappearance of Christ in the Etheric* (SteinerBooks, 2003)

- Three Initiates, *The Kybalion: A Study of the Hermetic Philosophy of Ancient Egypt and Greece* (Merchant Books, 2013)

- Yogi Ramacharaka, *Advanced Course in Yogi Philosophy and Oriental Occultism* (Cosimo Inc., 2006)

- Yogi Ramacharaka, *Lessons in Gnani Yoga: The Yoga of Wisdom* (Yogi Publication Society, 1934)

- Yogi Ramacharaka, *Raja Yoga or Mental Development* (Yogi Publication Society, 1934)

OTHER BOOKS BY

RON MACFARLANE

THERE IS a puzzling and pervasive misconception in present-day thinking that the existence of God cannot be intellectually determined, and that mentally accepting the existence of God is strictly a matter of non-rational belief (faith).

As such, contemplating God's existence is erroneously regarded as the exclusive subject of faith-based or speculative ideologies (religion and philosophy) which have no proper place in natural scientific study.

The fact is, there are a number of very convincing intellectual arguments concerning the existence of God that have been around for hundreds of years. Indeed, the existence of God can be determined with compelling intellectual certainty—provided the thinker honestly wishes to do so. Moreover, recent advances and discoveries in science have not weakened previous intellectual arguments for God's existence, but instead have enormously strengthened and supported them.

Intellectually assenting to the existence of God is easily demonstrated to be a superlatively logical conclusion, not some vague irrational conceptualization. Remarkably, at the present time there are only two seriously-competing intellectual explanations of life: the existence of God (the "God-hypothesis") and the existence of infinite universes (the "multiverse theory"). The postulation of an infinite number of unobservable universes is clearly a desperate attempt by atheistic scientists to avoid the God-hypothesis as the most credible and logical intellectual explanation of life and the universe. Moreover, under intellectual scrutiny, the scientifically celebrated "evolutionary theory" is here demonstrated to be fatally-flawed (philosophically illogical) as a credible explanation of life.

In this particular discourse, five well-known intellectual arguments for God's existence will be thoroughly examined. In considering these arguments, every attempt has been made to include current contributions, advances and discoveries that have modernized the more traditional arguments. Prior to examining these particular arguments for God, the universal predilection to establish intellectual 'oneness'—"monism"—will be considered in detail as well as the recurring propensity to postulate the existence of one supreme being—"monotheism."

Once intellectual certainty of one Supreme Being is established, a number of divine attributes can be logically deduced as well. Eleven of these attributes will be determined and examined in greater detail.

This book is available to order from Amazon.com

FROM DARKNESS TO LIGHT

FOR COUNTLESS esoteric students today, the Mystery centres of ancient times have retained a powerful and fascinating allure. Moreover, there is often a wishful longing to revive and continue their secretive initiatory activity into modern times.

Unfortunately, this anachronistic longing is largely based on an illusionary misunderstanding of these Mysteries and the real reasons for their destined demise.

The primary reason for the disappearance of the ancient Mysteries is that they have been supplanted by the superior new mysteries—the mysteries of the Son. These new mysteries were initiated by Christ-Jesus himself. In order to better understand these Son-mysteries in a spiritually-scientific way, Rudolf Steiner (1861–1925) established the Anthroposophical Movement and Society.

Unfortunately, anthroposophy today has become unduly influenced by members and leaders who long to transform spiritual science into a modern-day Mystery institution. Moreover, contrary to his own words and intentions, Rudolf Steiner is even claimed to be the founder of some new "Michael-Mysteries."

By carefully establishing a correct esoteric understanding of the ancient pagan Mysteries, as well as a better appreciation of the new mysteries of the Son, this well-researched and readable discourse convincingly shows that all current and past attempts to revive the ancient pagan Mysteries regressively diverts human development backward to the seducer of mankind, Lucifer, rather than progressively forward to the saviour of mankind, Christ-Jesus.

Moreover, by additionally tracing the intriguing historical

OTHER BOOKS

development of esoteric Christianity (particularly the Knights of the Holy Grail and Rosicrucianism) alongside Freemasonry, the Knights Templar and Theosophy, this important and necessary study illuminates the correct esoteric position and true significance of anthroposophical spiritual science.

This book is available to order from Amazon.com

THE PRIDE OF civilized mankind—intellectual thinking—is at a critical crossroads today. No doubt surprising to many, the cognitive capacity to consciously formulate abstract ideas in the mind, and then to manipulate them according to devised rules of logic in order to acquire new knowledge has only been humanly possible for about the last 3,000 years. Prior to intellectual (abstract) thinking, mental activity characteristically consisted of vivid pictorial images that arose spontaneously in the human mind from natural and supernatural stimuli.

The ability to think abstractly is the necessary foundation for mathematics, language and empirical science. The developmental history of intellectual thought, then, exactly parallels the developmental history of mathematics, language and science. Moreover, since abstract thinking inherently encourages the cognitive separation of subject (the thinker) and object (the perceived environment), the history of intellectual development also parallels the historical development of self-conscious (ego) awareness.

Over the last 3000 years, mankind in general has slowly perfected intellectual thinking; and thereby developed complex mathematics, sophisticated languages, comprehensively-detailed empirical sciences and pronounced ego-awareness. Unfortunately, all this intellectual activity over the many previous centuries has also exclusively strengthened human awareness of the physical, material world and substantially decreased awareness of the superphysical spiritual world.

That is why today, intellectual thinking is at a critical crossroads in further development. Thinking (intellectual or otherwise) is a superphysical activity—an activity within the soul. Empirical science is incorrect in postulating that physical brain tissue generates thought. The brain is simply the biological "sending and receiving" apparatus: sending sense-perceptions to the soul and receiving thought-conceptions from the soul. All this activity certainly generates chemical and electrical activity within the brain; but this activity is the effect, not the cause of thinking.

The danger to future intellectual thought is that increased acceptance of the erroneous scientific notion that thinking is simply brain-chemistry will increasingly deny and deaden true superphysical thinking. Future thinking runs the risk of becoming "a self-fulfilled prophecy"—the more people fervently believe that thought is simply brain-chemistry, the more thought will indeed become simply brain-chemistry. As a result, future human beings will be less responsible for generating their own thinking activity and more involuntarily controlled by their own brain chemistry. The artificial intelligence of machines won't become more human; but instead human beings will become more like robotic machines.

Presently, then, empirical science is leading intellectual thinking in a downward, materialistic direction. Correspondingly, however, true spiritual science (anthroposophy) is also actively engaged in leading intellectual thought back to its superphysical source in the soul. *Physical Science to Spiritual Science: the Future Development of Intellectual Thought* begins by examining the historical development of intellectual thinking and the corresponding rise of physical science. Once this has been discussed, practical and detailed information is presented on how spiritual science is leading intellectual thinking back to its true soul-source. It is intended that upon completion of this discourse, sincere and open-minded readers will themselves come to experience the exhilarating, superphysical nature of their own intellectual thought.

This book is available to order from Amazon.com

THE DIVINE TRINITY—the greatest of all Christian mysteries. How is it that the one God is a unity of three divine persons? Christ-Jesus first revealed this mystery to his disciples when on earth. Later, around the sixth century, the Trinitarian mystery was theologically clarified and outlined by the formulation of the Athanasian Creed.

Conceptual understanding of the divine Trinity has changed very little in Western society since then. Similarly with the theological understanding of the Logos-Word, as mentioned in the Gospel of St. John. The traditional understanding, that has remained essentially unchallenged for centuries, is that the Logos-Word is synonymous with God the Son. As for creation, the best that mainstream Christianity has historically provided is an ancient, allegorical account contained in the Book of Genesis.

Out of the hidden well-springs of esoteric Christianity, and as the title indicates, *The Greater Mysteries of the Divine Trinity, the Logos-Word and Creation*, delves much more deeply into the profound mysteries of the Trinitarian God, the Logos-Word of St. John and the creation of the universe. The divine Trinity is here demonstrated to be the loving union of Heavenly Father, Holy Mother and Eternal Son. The Logos-Word is here evidenced to be the "Universal Man," the primordial cosmic creation of God the Son. Universal creation itself is here detailed to be the "one life becoming many"—the multiplication of the Logos-Word into countless individualized life-forms and beings.

The depth and breadth of original and thought-provoking

OTHER BOOKS

information presented here will, no doubt, stimulate and excite those esoteric thinkers who are seriously seeking answers to the deeper mysteries of life, existence and the universe.

This book is available to order from Amazon.com

WHEN CHRIST-JESUS walked the earth over two thousand years ago, he established a two-fold division in his teaching that has continued to this day. To the general public, he simplified his teaching and presented it in pictorial, allegorical and figurative imagery in the form of stories, parables and lessons that could be imaginatively and intuitively understood.

To his inner circle of disciples (who were sufficiently prepared), however, he taught intellectual concepts, clear ideas and logical reasoning that could be understood on a much deeper and wider level of comprehension. As biblically explained:

> Then the disciples came and said to him, "Why do you speak to them [the general public] in parables?" And he answered them, "To you it has been given to know the secrets of the kingdom of heaven, but to them it has not been given … This is why I speak to them in parables, because seeing they do not see, and hearing they do not hear, nor do they understand." (Matt 13:10, 13)

Moreover, in union with the divine, Our Saviour was able to reveal sacred knowledge that had never been previously presented in the entire history of mankind: "I will explain mysteries hidden since the creation of the world" (Matt 13:35). This sacred and revealed knowledge has been termed "Christ-mysteries" or "mysteries of the Son."

After his glorious resurrection and ascension, Christ-Jesus institutionalized his two-fold mystery-teachings through St. Peter and St. John (the evangelist, not the apostle). Through St. Peter, Our Saviour instituted a universal Christian *religion* and *theology* to preserve, promote and convey the more basic and simplified mystery-teachings that are intended for the general public. Through St. John, Christ-Jesus instituted a universal Christian *philosophy* and *theosophy* to preserve, promote and convey the more comprehensive and complex mystery-teachings that are intended for the more advanced disciples (Christian initiates). In esoteric terminology, the institutionalized teachings through St. Peter are known as the "lesser mysteries of exoteric Christianity." The institutionalized teachings through St. John are known as the "greater mysteries of esoteric Christianity."

While both mystery-teaching approaches are equally sacred, profound and intended to complement each other, corrupt and intolerant authorities within the universal institution (Church) of St. Peter, for many centuries, persecuted and attacked any public expressions of esoteric Christianity. Consequently, genuine historical forms of esoteric Christianity, such as the Knights of the Holy Grail and the Fraternity of the Rose-Cross, were forced to be secretive and publically-hidden during the past two thousand years.

Thankfully today, the social, political and intellectual climate has progressed to the point where the greater mystery-teachings of esoteric Christianity can begin to be publically revealed for the first time. This modern-day outpouring really began with the twentieth-century establishment of anthroposophy by Rudolf Steiner (1861–1925). The information and approach presented in *The Star of Higher Knowledge: The Five Guiding Mysteries of Esoteric Christianity* is intended to augment and continue the mystery-teachings of Christ-Jesus as safeguarded by the Rosicrucian Fraternity and publicized through anthroposophy.

Consequently, this particular discourse delves much more deeply and comprehensively into the cosmos-changing salvational achievement of Christ-Jesus: the historical and cosmic preparations; as well as his birth, life, death, resurrection and ascension. While much of this mystery information may be unfamiliar, unknown and unexpected to mainstream (exoteric) Christianity, it in no way is meant to criticize, denigrate or displace the profound teachings of the universal Church; but rather, to complement, to enhance and to enlarge—for the betterment of true Christianity and, thereby, the betterment of all mankind.

This book is available to order from Amazon.com

OTHER BOOKS

Also check out the authour's website:

www.heartofshambhala.com

A Site Dedicated to True Esoteric Christianity

Contemporary Christianity, the world religion established by the God-Man, Christ-Jesus, and founded on the revelatory-principle that "God is love," is hardly the shining example of ideological unity and universal brotherhood that it was intended to be. There are approximately 41,000 different Christian denominations in the world today, many of which are fervently hostile to each other.

Atheistic and anti-Christian polemicists have concluded that there is something inherently wrong with Christianity itself and, in consequence, it is doomed to failure and eventual extinction.

Discerning Christian advocates, however, know that any apparent failure to realize the high ideals of Christianity is not due to the profound teachings and the illustrious life-example of Christ-Jesus, but instead to the limitations of wounded human nature. Corrupt, power-hungry, destructive and evil-minded human beings have twisted, distorted and fragmented true Christianity for the past two thousand years, and continue to do so today.

Moreover, on a much deeper spiritual level, since Christianity is indeed a divinely-initiated endeavor to help restore "fallen" humanity, powerful and demonic beings have attempted to destroy nascent Christianity from its very inception. But thankfully, according to Christ-Jesus himself, "the powers of hell will not prevail against it [Christianity]" (Matt 16:18).

Sadly contributing to the injurious fragmentation of Christianity—the "religion of divine love"—is the sectarian hostility between certain proponents of anthroposophy and select members of the Catholic Church. In both cases, this is largely due to ignorance; that is, an almost complete lack of understanding about the true significance and mission of the other—anthroposophical critics know almost nothing of Catholicism, and Catholic critics know almost nothing about anthroposophy.

The wonderful reconciliatory fact is that anthroposophy and Catholicism are not conflicting polar opposites, but are instead like two sides of the same golden coin—different, but complementary. Instead of only one side or the other being the only true approach to Christ-Jesus, both are uniquely necessary and both positively contribute to the complete truth of Christianity.

Since this author is happily and harmoniously both an anthroposophist and a Catholic, *The Greater and Lesser Mysteries of Christianity: The Complementary Paths of Anthroposophy and Catholicism* earnestly seeks to correct the misinformation and lack of understanding that each partisan critic has for the other. As in almost every significant dispute, increased knowledge and familiarity about each other will in time bring both sides closer together for mutual growth and benefit.

This book is available to order from Amazon.com

www.ingramcontent.com/pod-product-compliance
Lightning Source LLC
Chambersburg PA
CBHW051343040426
42453CB00007B/379